CATCH A FIRE

Fuelling Inquiry and Passion Through Project-Based Learning

EDITED BY
MATT HENDERSON

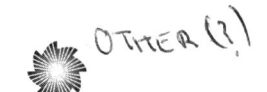

PORTAGE & MAIN PRESS

© 2019 by Portage & Main Press

Pages of this publication may be reproduced under licence from Access Copyright or with the express written permission of Portage & Main Press, or as permitted by law.

All rights are otherwise reserved and no part of this publication may be reproduced, stored in a retrieval system, or transmitted in any form or by any means—electronic, mechanical, photocopying, scanning, recording or otherwise—except as specifically authorized.

Portage & Main Press gratefully acknowledges the financial support of the Province of Manitoba through the Department of Sport, Culture & Heritage and the Manitoba Book Publishing Tax Credit, and the Government of Canada through the Canada Book Fund (CBF) for our publishing activities.

Printed and bound in Canada by Friesens
Illustration, cover and chapter openers, by Jessica Fortner
Design by Relish New Brand Experience

Library and Archives Canada Cataloguing in Publication

Title: Catch a fire : fuelling inquiry and passion through project-based learning / Matt A. Henderson, editor.
Names: Henderson, Matt A., 1975- editor.
Identifiers: Canadiana 20189066385 | ISBN 9781553797517 (softcover)
Subjects: LCSH: Project method in teaching.
Classification: LCC LB1027.43 .C38 2019 | DDC 371.3/6—dc23

Also issued in electronic format:

978-1-55379-789-0 (PDF)
978-1-55379-790-6 (e-PUB)

22 21 20 19   1 2 3 4 5

SEVEN OAKS EDUCATION FOUNDATION is an organization dedicated to providing the students of Seven Oaks School Division access to post-secondary education. SOEF envisions a supportive community where all students believe they can continue their education and training beyond high school.

The Foundation raises funds to help students realize their post-secondary goals through scholarship opportunities and distributes these funds to facilitate learning for as many students as possible.

Members of the Foundation engage the Seven Oaks community in actively supporting the post-secondary experience and counts on public support for continued success.

All proceeds from this book are donated to the Seven Oaks Education Foundation.

PORTAGE & MAIN PRESS

1-800-667-9673
www.portageandmainpress.com
Winnipeg, Manitoba
Treaty 1 Territory and homeland of the Métis Nation

This book is dedicated to the outstanding learners
who have changed our lives and the course
of the human experience on this planet.
Thank you for naming the world.

CONTENTS

Foreword vii

Preface ix

Introduction 1

1. What Is a Project? 7
   Matt Henderson

2. How Does Project-Based Learning Allow for the Development of the Whole Student? 13
   Tom Lake and Bonnie Powers

3. How Can Teachers Engage Students with Specific Learning Outcomes (SLOs) While Still Remaining True to the Spirit of Inquiry? 29
   Dave Law

4. What Can We Learn When We Live the Math? 45
   Glenys MacLeod

5. Insights from a Central American Agro-Conservation International Development Project 73
   Laura Sims

6. How Can Projects Work for Our Most Vulnerable Learners? 91
   Keith Fulford and Jonathan Dueck

7. How Can Project-Based Learning Work with Learners on the Autism Spectrum? 105
   Matt Henderson

8. Getting People on Board the Project-Based Learning Bus 129
   Sid Williamson

9. Experiencing Project-Based Learning: Beginning in Teacher Education 135
   Theresa Armstrong and Dr. Eva Brown

10. Ecological Literacy and Project-Based Learning.......................149
    Will Burton

11. One House Many Nations: Indigenous Project-Based Collaboration 171
    Alex Wilson and Jacob Mans

12. Home-School Projects: Are They Learning the Right Stuff?.............187
    Bonnie Ferguson-Baird

Conclusion: Assessment for Continuity..................................201
    Bonnie Powers and Tom Lake; Glenys MacLeod; Will Burton;
    Bonnie Ferguson-Baird; Laura Sims; Matt Ferguson

FOREWORD

As educators we can sometimes be alarmingly slow on the uptake. We see things and know things, but somehow, we don't connect them with our teaching practice.

For longer than I've been a teacher (and that's been a while) we've known about the power of extracurricular activities. Students and caring adults spend a ton of time and energy on sports, in the arts, and in social-justice work. They do so not for money or marks but for the joy of the activity itself, for the connection to others, for the opportunity to accomplish something that has meaning for them and the world. Extracurricular activities are real. Whether it's a team, a production, or Gay-Straight Alliance; students are working for something real: to win a game, entertain an audience, or change the world. They evaluate their effort in the real world, learn from the experience, and then figure out how to get better.

We should learn from this. In *Catch a Fire*, Matt Henderson and his colleagues are doing exactly that: building rich, powerful learning opportunities for students through engaging project-based inquiry. The stories of teaching and learning in this volume attest to the power of project-based learning. As they do in extracurricular activities, students put tremendous time and energy into their tasks, they become actors in the real world, and they find community as learners. They find their passion, and that passion builds their unique identity and helps them find their place in the world. And it sure beats copying notes and doing worksheets.

We often justify boring learning experiences in school as we do cough syrup. It may not taste great, but it works. It's necessary for you and you'll thank us later. But in reality, we don't know what's coming later. We didn't know we'd experience the profound changes to our lives that information technology has wrought. And in retrospect, the changes we've seen have had more to do with the project-based, extracurricular learning of the likes of Bill Gates and Steve Jobs than from formal sequenced instruction.

Thanks to Matt Henderson and his colleagues for helping us to appreciate the power and possibility of inquiry-driven project-based learning and helping us figure out how to do it well.

Brian O'Leary
Superintendent, Seven Oaks School Division

PREFACE

This book is for all educators. It is for K-12 educators, higher-ed educators, and home schoolers. It is intended to provide insight into how projects are used in diverse ways in order to cultivate deep inquiry and curiosity.

This book came about because there seemed to be a dearth of project-based learning books that focused on the relationship between the learner and the educator. Many PBL books seem to focus heavily on the stages and processes of planning a project – which is a worthwhile subject – but many educators are seeking models of PBL where the learner is ultimately the project. In lieu of writing the book myself, I tapped into my network and asked master teachers I've encountered along my journey to contribute to the book.

As the editor, I would like to acknowledge the deep insight offered by the educators in this book. They are master educators who care about one thing: creating powerful learning experiences for learners so as to enable everyone on this planet to flourish.

I would also like to thank the folks at Portage & Main Press. From the beginning, Annalee, Catherine, and Garry have been invaluable advocates for this book and have provided critical advice and exerted incredible patience.

INTRODUCTION

Recently, I saw an online post about an app that enables students to reflect via video on their learning as a means of assessment for, as, and of learning itself. Yes, Recap is a very cool app I have found useful within my learning communities as a platform to capture point-in-time feedback from learners who have been working on various projects. The post is a blog entry from an elementary school teacher who talks about her courageous attempt to introduce project-based learning within her learning community, a Grade 3 and 4 class.

In the post, the educator describes how she introduced PBL, or project-based learning, to her students, and the step-by-step process she took that culminated in the use of Recap. It's amazing to see educators boosting their technique and method, but I noticed a glaring omission in her narrative – that is, why? Why adopt project-based learning as a means for learning and teaching?

By no means do I wish to throw this educator under the school bus. In fact, she should be commended for wanting to cultivate the interest and passion of her students. It's truly remarkable that she speaks to "essential questions" and that PBL might produce a certain level of authenticity in terms of the project and its assessment.

But what's missing, as I often find within the realm of PBL, is a reason why projects are a better or even viable alternative to what might be considered more traditional avenues to educate people. I use the term *alternative* loosely here, as someone who teaches at a school that people often refer to as "alternative."

When friends ask me if the Maples Met School, a Big Picture Learning school, is an alternative school, I often respond with something like: "The Maples Met School is a project-based school and a learner-centred school. Our species has been learning through projects for the past several thousands of years, so I would suggest that stacking kids in rows, feeding them content that has little to do with their experience, and then asking them to spit it back might be the most alternative system I could imagine." By the way, I am a huge hit at dinner parties.

As you can tell, I think about learning and projects a great deal, and I've developed a technique and pedagogy that is vigorously bathed in relationships, curiosity, and transformation. That said, it's taken me a considerable amount of time to realize why projects are indeed viable, and can sometimes produce deeper and richer educative experiences than the desks-in-rows model. I acknowledge that I make mistakes all the time, and I often have to apologize to learners and colleagues for these mistakes. I also acknowledge that there are outstanding educators who are perfectly captivating and engaging without subscribing to a project-based methodology. My line of reasoning is that, if learners envision projects in a specific way, they may feel empowered and discover that these learning experiences create robust neurological connections that ultimately change the physiology of their brains and lead to transformation.

Project-based learning can thus be articulated as a technique for teaching and learning. PBL at its best needs to be defined as both a teaching and learning methodology whereby learners are encouraged to follow their curiosity and passion in authentic, multidisciplinary, and rigorous ways. The design of PBL within any learning community should focus on allowing learners to channel their inquiry into hands-on experience, reflect on their progress, offer a substantial solution to a legitimate problem, and launch this solution into the world through a public exhibition of knowledge. Projects and project-based learning are fundamental ways in which we can question what it means to be human. What it means to be alive. This is the test. Do my learners feel alive, awakened, honoured, and valued during their time with me?

But before we dive into the hows and whys of PBL, we need to take a step back and do two things. First, we need to contemplate the purpose of education and who it serves. Second, we need to look at what we mean by educative experience. Without grasping these two concepts, entering into a project-based learning (or any kind of learning) foundation will produce, at best, arbitrary results and, at worst, a great deal of wasted time and energy. The latter result should not occur. The stakes are simply far too high.

So let's begin with what we believe is the purpose of education. If we're not constantly contemplating the purpose of education or the reason why we're educators, then any engagement with learners will be inadequate, directionless, and potentially damaging. If you're reading this, you clearly care about your learners, the fate of our species, and those other species and systems with which we interact and depend on, and you have a firm grip on why you became an educator. It's a calling. Not a vocation or a job. You work until you drop. You work through the summer, you visit families on the weekend, you haven't eaten lunch in decades, and you bawl your eyes out when your learners move on. You don't have time for petty interoffice gossip, you coach at 5:00 AM, and you rarely see the sun. In other words, you care! You care deeply about this thing we call education and, more importantly, you care about your learners.

There are a variety of ideological hooks upon which we can hang our hats. Some might suggest that education is about preparing students for the future, as if we have crystal balls to consult. Some might suggest that our task is to pass along cultural norms and expectations. Others might suggest that education serves as a means to create productive citizens who vote, pay taxes, abide by laws, and generally keep the peace. Education can also be a means to the good life, however we may wish to qualify this. For some, that means a house in the suburbs, one or more SUVs, and frequent trips to Ikea. For Aristotle, it might involve a fancy word like "eudaimonia," something along the lines of a flourishing of activity of the rational soul in accordance with virtue.

Education can provide a means for allocating the time and space for learners to ask deep existential questions about the universe and their place within it. What could be more important? What could be more critical than fostering a curiosity in a person so that they can ask powerful questions like, "What is the meaning of my life?", "What happens when I die?", and "What the heck is dark matter!?" At project-based schools, as you will see in the chapters ahead, learning is about cultivating the whole child, adult, or community. The learner is ultimately the project and the goal is to create opportunities for learners to flourish, to fall in love with the arts, science, mathematics, humanities, music, and life itself. Think Galileo, Leonardo, Jobs, or Musk. Think of that neighbour who is curious about everything and just seems to appreciate life.

Educators who seek to use PBL as a platform for transformation and growth are a rare breed. Learning *for* transformation and learning *as* transformation require, as Jack Mezirow suggests, processes through which we question many concepts we take at face value so that we can come closer to the truth and achieve more informed action. This, presumably, is the quest and challenge we all signed up for when we became educators. As such, you can see a PBL educator walking from a kilometre away. Right away, you notice that they care deeply about learners within their community and about learning. They're never satisfied with teaching the same skills and knowledge the same way to different learners. They respect the experience of each and every individual they encounter, and they aim to enter into a real dialogue with their students. They come to school every day ready to nurture the curiosity and creativity of each and every one of their learners. They're learner-centred and they realize that the stakes are high. They care, they're incredibly resourceful, and they're unbelievably creative. They also understand how to design an educative experience.

Viktor Frankl pushed this idea of education as a pursuit of experiences, questions, and life's meaning when he suggested, "Was Du erlebst, kann keine Macht der Welt Dir rauben." (What you have experienced, no power on earth can take from you.) All that we have on this rock hurtling through space is our experience. As John Dewey, Paulo Freire, David A. Kolb, and others have posited over time, a critical function of our task as educators is to deeply understand the experience of our learners in order to design future *educative* experiences for our learners. This means we need to get to know our learners. We need to democratize our learning communities, creating time and space for their experience to drive the learning. This is the power of projects. As educators, we can leverage the experience and inquiry of learners to open a world beyond the limits of what was previously conceived. We can initiate the spark to ignite passion and inquiry within the learner.

Sparking curiosity and encouraging inquiry about ourselves and the universe is what some might call critical thinking, but it also creates meaning. Meaning for our time on this planet, meaning for our relationships with each other and the biosphere, and meaning in the truth we seek. What if we all thought deeply about our purpose and tried to take meaningful, informed action to find it? With that sense of purpose, would we knowingly destroy our home planet, attack our neighbours, or willingly let people starve?

This deep contemplation also requires extensive content knowledge and an ability to think in many different ways. If you are going to contemplate the universe, you'd better be a mathematician, a historian, a geologist, a philosopher, an artist, and an athlete. Experience hones our skills and knowledge whenever we undertake good projects – but more on that later from the courageous educators who have come together to create this project.

This book came about as most good projects do – out of curiosity and a desire to deeply understand something that needs greater understanding. In my early career as an elementary school teacher (and I should write a letter of apology to all those students), I was engaged in primitive teaching that had me trying to take a massive body of knowledge and present it to rows of 10-year-olds on a daily basis. What I discovered through this process, after years of reflection, was that the most beneficial educative experience came about when my learners and I were engaged in something that captured our curiosity, something that brought us together, and something that was real. This was my first inkling of the power of PBL.

Later on in my career, I began to document the time when project work was truly educative. I began to pinpoint, with the help of my incredible teaching partners, when we'd struck gold and when we had missed the mark. We knew that learner-centred projects could help learners pursue their passion and stimulate inquiry, connecting them with experts in the field, praising their final product and solution, and launching their results into the world. We also discovered there was a difference between deep and powerful learning and simply going through the motions of PBL (something of which I have been incredibly guilty). I wanted to learn more about PBL, but there simply wasn't anything out there beyond a few websites and skinny books that employed a cookie-cutter approach.

So instead of rooting around for tips and tricks that master teachers use to engage learners with projects, I decided to badger some of the best educators I know from around the world to help me create a book. I've seen many of them in action. I wanted to harness their wisdom and glean what I could from their passion, their love of learners, and their desire to fundamentally make the world better. Each chapter in this book was written by a different educator (or educators) whose passion blazes across the page. These educators live project-based learning, whether they acknowledge it or not. They listen to their learners. They challenge their learners. They care about their learners.

The chapters in this book seek to question not only the *how* of project-based learning but, perhaps more importantly, the *what* and the *why*. You'll notice how these master educators always come back to the essential element: the learner and the experience of the learner. These authors, whether public school teachers, homeschoolers, university professors, or rogue shepherds, come at teaching and learning with their own curiosity, passion, and desire to connect with other humans. Their writing and thinking is saturated with empathy, expertise, a desire to do better, and an acknowledgment of their need to collaborate with others.

Unlike some books about project-based learning, this one won't offer the reader a step-by-step or itemized process for doing projects. Rather, these chapters offer insight into how connecting with our learners, honouring their experience, and turning what was once taken at face value into deep and rich questioning, can lead to powerful life-changing projects.

Our hope is that this book can be used in a few different ways. First, read the whole thing through from beginning to end. Then leave it alone. Think. Reflect. Come back to it and explore individual chapters that challenged you, inspired you, or frustrated you. Contact the authors, have colleagues read your copy and provide feedback, and read it again.

Second, revisit the chapters that are important to you. Borrow, steal, and reinvent what each author has done. Go back to your learning community and experiment with similar ideas. Turn your attention to your learners' experience for a day. What did you find out? Propose and design a project! Try something new.

Third, skim the book and leave it on the bus, or in a tidy bathroom.

Last, do all of the above and then write your own book, blog, or journal. Reflect on whether or not you have experienced PBL or not. What challenges have you faced, what successes have you had, and what do you truly believe about learning and teaching? Our hope is that this book will soon bear all the battle scars: pencil marks, stickies, ideas, and notes-to-self that will inspire others to create the next edition. These chapters are simply *our* understanding of how we connect with learners and try to further their inquiry. Challenge us. Engage us. Inspire us.

In this book, you will meet some of the most talented and passionate educators I've encountered. I thank them for sharing their experiences, which are inspiring, meaningful, and truly priceless.

—M.H.

References

Dewey, John. (1938). *Education and experience.* New York, NY: The MacMillan Company.

Frankl, Viktor. (1959.) *Man's search for meaning.* Boston, MA: Beacon Press.

Freire, Paulo. (1970). *Pedagogy of the oppressed.* New York, NY: The Seabury Press.

Kolb, David A. (1984). *Experiential learning : Experience as the source of learning and development.* Engelwood Cliffs, NJ: Prentice-Hall.

Mezirow, Jack. (2000). *Learning as transformation: Critical perspectives on a theory in progress.* San Francisco, CA: Jossey-Bass.

CHAPTER 1
What Is a Project?

Matt Henderson, Assistant Superintendent, Seven Oaks School Division, and former principal, Maples Met School
Winnipeg, Manitoba, Canada

For this chapter, I asked learners of all ages to tell me what they think a project is. These learners, both young and old, all do amazing projects. They push the idea of what it means to be human on a daily basis. They are offbeat, yes, but they ask deep questions about the universe; they question their role within it; their curiosity is unquenchable.

Joel Jae Serrano, High School Learner

I would consider my childhood unconventional. Living in Dubai did not help either. The costs of living meant that my family barely made any allowance; therefore, I never had many toys. So I created my own. That was probably my magical moment – my very first project.

I think a project is something that has a purpose, triggered by an idea or a question that we have stumbled upon during our day-to-day lives. A broad question like, "How can we reform capitalism?", or something as simple as, "Why are there labels on our store-bought fruits?" I like to think of it with a stoic's perspective, instead of asking nonessential questions and thinking they matter in the real world. A project requires a set of tasks to accomplish, challenging our limitations. Creativity arises from working within these limitations, and constraints placed on these projects is also key.

A proverb from Joi Ito, director of the MIT Media Lab, goes as follows: "Education is what people do to you. Learning is what you do to yourself." When I heard this, I realized that I was no longer a student but my own teacher. The point was not to receive a greater education, but to create my own learning and shape it for the unique challenges that await in this complex, unpredictable world, which is more connected than ever before.

Dr. Jay Roberts, PhD, Professor of Education, Earlham College

When we speak about project-based learning, we often have mental models in our heads about what such a pedagogy entails. But it is important to speak a bit about what we mean by a project in order to fully realize its educative potential. After all, a project poorly conceptualized with substandard planning is doomed from the start – regardless of the quality of the teacher and students.

For me, an educative project must contain five central elements:

1. Open-ended framing. (If the project is about gardens, do my learners know what a garden is?)
2. Authentic context. (Are my learners going to be engaged in gardening?)
3. Rich content. (Are my learners going to be learning about cell division, photosynthesis, nitrogen cycles, etc., from experts in the field?)
4. Intentional scaffolding. (Are there critical moments when we connect with the learners to ensure that they are learning?)
5. Student ownership. (Do the learners own what they are learning? Is the project their own?)

Projects should be *open-ended* in the sense that the design and conceptualization of the project are not predetermined in advance by the teacher. This takes an artful balance between laying the groundwork and framing the project without over-determining the design to the point that students perceive the project as "handed down" rather than co-constructed.

Projects should incorporate *authentic contexts*. The project should matter to someone besides the teacher and the students. This can be done through a presentation of learning to a community partner or through careful framing and facilitation that enables students to see the connections between the project and their lived experiences.

The *content* associated with the project should be rich and *intentionally scaffolded* (or integrated) through direct instruction, activities, and assessments. We must guard against the false dichotomies of lecture vs. active learning. That is, it is okay for our learners to engage in lectures. They are not bad, nor are other ways of connecting with content. We are after content that offers a rich, meaningful learning experience, and this can be achieved through a variety of instructional methodologies – including direct instruction.

Finally, projects should put the *student at the centre* of the learning endeavour. Students should be actively involved in all aspects of the project, including design, implementation, and assessment.

Alyric Balcita, High School Learner

A project can really be almost anything. If there's a question you really want to know the answer to, and it involves a process, you can turn that into a project. If there is something you really want to do or prove, that can also be a project!

A project comes with passion and drive. Without those two things, wouldn't the project seem pointless? Of course, every project has a purpose, but without passion or drive, there would be no positive motivation. That is what pushes you to complete it. Sometimes we're given projects that we don't enjoy. When it comes to that, we have to find something in the project that will help us complete it. For instance, the longer you take to get it done, the longer you have to dread it! With project-based learning, everything is project-based (obviously). When almost everything you do is in project form, you get better at finding ways to get motivated.

I think that the best projects are based on something you enjoy. If a final product is something that can be made from or presented about something you're passionate about, then you've found that drive. When it's something you enjoy, you put in more effort without thinking too hard about it. That is what a project is to me.

Kal Barteski, Artist

For me, a project is a meaningful, creation-based task or series of tasks, like a painting or a collection of paintings. There is a goal, but the goal can be loosely defined. It is a thing that gains momentum, meaning, and focus – maybe magic, too.

Sometimes the start and end of such works are clearly marked. Sometimes there are parameters and requirements. The "projects" I gravitate toward and dream about are organic processes that change shape and scope as the work progresses and interacts with the world. One example that speaks to this is the SeaWalls Churchill project I was part of in Churchill, Manitoba <www.seawallschurchill.ca>. This project brought together artists from all over the world to a community in need. I love this description of the SeaWalls project:

> SeaWalls Churchill was created with the intention to educate and inspire a community to protect the oceans, but what transpired was more powerful than that. It was the story of a devastated small town on the edge of the Arctic being reminded of their own value and worthiness in this world.

Kevin Nikkel, Filmmaker

Speaking as an independent filmmaker, a project for me is a documentary. I understand each project as a process. When an idea triggers my curiosity, I'm compelled towards understanding something. I formulate my discovery into a summation of my learning, which is a finished film. To do this, I dive deep into what others have discovered previously. That involves lots of reading and hours spent in the archives, searching for clues. I'll travel to a location, try and uncover a source, and find people with answers to my questions.

Film projects are about collaboration. I seek out those with wisdom and a connection to the story I want to tell – with luck they'll be willing to appear on camera. Equally important are the friends I return to, film after film, who help me bring the story into focus. A camera operator, a composer, or friends who patiently watch a draft of a latest project – they know my body of work, they know where I've been, and they know when I'm starting to lose objectivity. I know that, as much as a project demands hours of introverted work, these projects are at their best when developed in the context of community.

Our consumer-driven culture usually sees projects as commodities needing to be measured and assessed. Did it get into enough big film festivals? Did it play on TV? How many "likes"? How many views online? This is a poor measure of a good project. I'd rather ask: Did I enjoy the collaborative process of learning, the process that is reflected in the end credits of the film? Did my film help others see something in a way they hadn't been able to see it before?

Dennis Littky, Co-founder, Big Picture Learning

A project can be good? A project can be bad?

The Big Picture philosophy goes beyond projects. First, it's all about the project being one the student is interested in and passionate about. Projects are better than lectures, but if they do not belong to the student, they have not gone far enough.

The goal is to engage students so that they want to study, want to go deeper, and find the flow in the work. Once students find out their interest and what they want to investigate or do, then it is important for a staff member to be a coach who helps students go deeper and helps them stay engaged with their idea.

I know there are many protocols to help students develop projects. But these are only helpful when the student cares. If the student doesn't care, then it's fake learning.

Yes, my schools in the past have done great projects based on the curriculum. But for 22 years, the emphasis, the key to a project is that students make it their own. One student was studying the Vietnam War because his father fought in it and wouldn't speak about it. This fact kept the student engaged and motivated him to take college classes, to have war veterans as his mentors, and even to visit Vietnam.

One boy's uncle was shot and killed in a bar. The killer was never caught, and the boy fought to have the legislators make sure all bars had video cameras at their doors. So you see, many projects can come about based on personal needs.

Projects are good. We can improve on how we help students develop them. But if they are not student-driven projects, then they are not good enough.

About the Authors
Tom Lake and Bonnie Powers are passionate experiential educators with experience in traditional (primary through higher) education, and outdoor, corporate, and environmental education programming. This husband and wife team travels to study and engage with different forms of education around the world. Their interests include learning, being outside, and thinking outside the box.

Who Should Read This Chapter?
Anyone interested in broadening their scope of practice to include socio-emotional development as well as academic progress.

The Theme of This Chapter in Three Words
Learners are people.

As an Educator, What Are You Passionate About?
The process of learning, engaging and empowering individuals, and valuing each learner as a unique person.

CHAPTER 2

How Does Project-Based Learning Allow for the Development of the Whole Student?

Tom Lake, Northwest Passage High School, and Bonnie Powers, Minnesota State University, Mankato, St. Paul, Minnesota, USA

Education is one of the great uniting, and potentially divisive, factors in life. Whatever our backgrounds are, people around the world have experience-based opinions about what education is and what it should be. The industrial era model of learning, characterized by timed lessons, rigid structures, and straight rows of desks, served its early 20th-century purpose by creating a relatively uniform workforce, but we now find ourselves in a new era where information is available at the touch of a fingertip, where young adults can expect to work a multitude of jobs rather than finding themselves locked into one stable career, and where adaptability is arguably more important than either knowledge or experience (Adkins, 2016). The disparity between classroom learning and current employment demands and expectations is illustrated by employers across the nation reporting that new employees lack important workplace skills (Dishman, 2016). These skills, which are primarily socio-emotional in nature – leadership, cooperation, teamwork, communication, dealing with adversity, and goal setting – are distinctive in making up a learner's toolbox for the 21st- and, potentially, 22nd-century workplace.

We began our own journey as educators in the outdoor and experiential education setting, and transitioned to the classroom from there. As such, our focus has always been on personal and socio-emotional learning. We believe that students should be encouraged to learn about themselves – their own strengths and weaknesses, how they learn and process, how to navigate life, and how to reflect, adapt, and develop these areas – in school. Project-based learning (PBL) can allow this balance of growing self-awareness while developing effective navigation strategies to emerge naturally. By making socio-emotional development as important as academic progress, PBL schools have the opportunity to recognize and support the whole learner because the freedom of this approach allows educators more time to focus on the individual student.

As educators, we know that every challenge our students face is messy, involving concepts from across subjects and generally necessitating social interaction. Project-based learning enables schools to move away from the sterility and impersonal aspects of single-subject classes, creating space for the study and experience of the messiness of our world in multi- and cross-disciplinary ways. Our experiences within a range of project-based schools in the United States have shown us that while PBL varies, the core elements of the Experiential Learning Cycle are consistent across practices. Learners engage in a process that includes concrete experience, reflective observation, abstract conceptualization, and active experimentation (Kolb, 1984). This is often condensed into a mantra of *plan, do, review, improve*.

While traditional schools often implement a similar process, transference of learning between subjects and skill sets is generally limited because of differences in curricular design and implementation (and a disconnect in how all of these subjects and skills are related). In the PBL environment, the primary concrete experience is relevant and applicable to the student's life. This gets student buy-in from the beginning, facilitating inquiry and curiosity that fuels the reflective observation phase, encouraging meaningful and applicable abstract conceptualization, and supporting students to actively experiment with the knowledge and skills they are developing. In addition, we can use Abraham Maslow's "hierarchy of needs" as a checklist of sorts to identify the basic needs of the learner (Maslow, 1943). There are a variety of such tools at our disposal, but we find that Maslow's hierarchy provides an easily accessible reminder of the broad needs and challenges that our students may be facing. Once identified, these needs can then be used as a template for developing individual progress plans, charting each learner's developmental progress, and collaboratively engineering individual and group projects.

In our work, we aim to facilitate safe environments for learners to practise navigating through the sometimes chaotic maze that is life. We meet students where they are, collaborate with them to help them identify where they want to go, and then work with them to progress in that direction. This requires us to engage the whole learner, facilitating targeted and overall skill development both academically and socio-emotionally while supporting the difficult transition to a new learning environment. There are significant challenges in being an educator – in the creating, organizing, motivating, and following through of daily function within a school as well as in the maintaining of a work-life balance, forming new relationships, and pursuing our own interests within our personal lives – but we hold ourselves to the same expectations we have of our students: that we will experience, reflect, learn, and adapt in order to overcome the obstacles we face.

We have seen firsthand how a holistic approach to PBL transcends the classroom to positively affect progress at school, at home, and socially. The following stories are composite portraits reflecting real experiences of students and staff from project-based schools that we have been associated with in North America. In these stories, we are examining three main concepts: the challenge of transitioning to the PBL environment, educating the whole learner, and helping learners develop effective toolboxes. We have changed names and identifying details in these stories to respect the privacy of individuals involved. In our usage, the term *we* refers to an experience involving one or both of the authors of this chapter.

Hear the Music

Julia struggled in traditional school. She needed more time to process concepts than she was allotted. She fell behind and, although she wanted to catch up, she thought that doing so was an impossible goal. Each subject would run away from her, getting harder and harder in what had become a never-ending chase. She gradually lost hope, and apathy set in. She wondered why she should try to do anything if she never succeeded. Her inaction was seen by others as negative behaviour, which compounded the impact of her low grades on her sense of self-worth. Her assumption that she could never be right was a product of the structure of the school system and was quickly becoming a self-fulfilling prophecy.

Julia and her parents began actively looking for an alternative school. She had known other people who had transferred to a project-based school in the area, and she decided to make the switch. When she began at the PBL school, she was a year behind in credit. Straightaway, she really enjoyed the educational environment and culture. However, she still struggled to take control of her own learning.

Creating an independent project was no easy matter. Julia was used to having very structured classes with her time filled up by worksheets. She had never been required to think about what to learn or how to break a project into tasks, having been assigned task after task (in linear fashion) by her teachers. She had difficulty picking a topic and identifying specific outcomes, and was overwhelmed by the amount of work and effort that was involved in actually doing a project on her own. She'd never before been asked what area she was interested in, or prompted to connect a school concept to her own interests. She'd never had to figure out how long a task would take because she'd always been assigned a time limit for every task. These skills take time to learn and practice, time that Julia had never had the opportunity to take before. Her confidence in her own abilities was so low that she did not believe that she could handle these challenges

In her first projects, she thought small and put in as little effort as possible, worried that she would make mistakes. She needed the staff to facilitate opportunities for her to regain her confidence. When we first sat down and worked with her, Julia wasn't very secure in herself. Identifying this issue helped us figure out what skills would help her progress as an individual, and not just as a student.

We asked her what her passions were, which high-school credits she was missing, and brainstormed with her how we could connect these with the parameters of a project. Julia loved electronic dance music (EDM) – not just listening to it, but also the production and history of the movement. In order to set Julia up for success, we strove to help her create a project that she could complete as well as enjoy. We collaborated with her to align this topic with standards in history, media, and digital art that could be covered, and then broke the project down step by step. Where should we finish? What would the final deliverable look like? What were some of the big questions that we wanted to find out? What kind of tasks would answer these questions? We discussed the questions in depth, working through each one until Julia determined what the final deliverable might look like. Julia decided that she would create an album that represented the EDM movement with landmark tracks and DJs.

We discussed what structure would work best to help her accomplish the tasks. Finding that a compartmentalized worksheet-type structure was comfortable for her, we put all of this information into a Google Classroom where Julia could easily access and record her progress.

After creating the plan and the structure for the project, we worked through the timeline. When do you think we should finish the entire project? How long will it take to do each task? Julia would automatically give herself a short time frame, while the staff would urge her to add more time. We worked back and forth, adjusting the timeline to allow for processing, reflection, and all of the other things that Julia had going on in her life, before coming to a consensus. There was ample time to allow for successful completion within a reasonable time frame, and we all knew when the deadlines were.

Every morning, we checked in. What are you planning on doing today? What are you looking forward to? How much time are you allocating? This encouraged Julia to get in the habit of breaking her tasks down into manageable portions of work. We'd check in again throughout the day. How's it going? This helped support Julia with her time management while giving us the opportunity to voice concerns and challenges. Once every few days, we would discuss what she had discovered since the last time. Through the Google Classroom setup, we already knew *what* she had been doing, so we focused more on what she had actually been *learning*. After she completed each task, we would meet to reflect and analyze her learning process thus far. Julia had grown accustomed to focusing on the negative aspects of her performance, so we intentionally focused on giving positive reinforcement to Julia based on her accomplishments.

This process wasn't entirely smooth. Julia had good days and bad days but, over time, the good ones started to outnumber the bad. The project lasted over a month, as Julia had other things going on at the same time. The consistency during this longer time frame helped to build and reinforce Julia's confidence. It wouldn't have had the same effect if we'd blasted through the project in a week. A longer time frame gave Julia time to reflect and time to apply the lessons from that reflection. When Julia presented the album, she could explain with confidence how and why she had created the album cover the way she did. She introduced each track and artist, explaining the significance of each particular piece of music within the EDM movement. She then conducted a Q&A session and answered the specific questions of her peers, allowing her to showcase how knowledgeable she had become about her interest.

In a way, this was a simple project. Completing the project didn't require addressing a long list of standards. Nor was there a huge amount of credit associated with that first project, but it gave Julia success in multiple areas, along with positive recognition from staff, peers, and also herself. She had the opportunity to see some of the things that she was good at. As well as feeling good about herself, she also gained confidence in trying to improve, in asking questions, in recognizing areas that needed improvement, and in trying new things regardless of the possibility of failure.

Through these gains in confidence and self-advocacy, she was able to gain autonomy. Over time, Julia started working on projects at home. The staff let her move at her own pace, giving her extended time for work. They gave her time to process, asking her questions and then giving her time to think them through rather than expecting answers right away. As time progressed, we were able to refer back to this first project as a baseline and a reminder of how she already had many of the skills to overcome challenges; she just needed to practice them.

The EDM project provided a jump-start – a spark of confidence. This was the first project that Julia was really passionate about. Not only did she learn how to use her strengths and interests in order to gain school credit, she also learned how to manage her time and maintain confidence in her abilities. After that, Julia worked with us to create a system that gave her time to process and successfully complete tasks of her own design while keeping to a high standard. Four months after Julia completed that first project, she ran a three-week electronic music production training workshop for her peers. She went on to build a sandbox speaker, an audio system that dampens the energy and lowers the resonant frequency of the speaker by transferring energy to grains of sand in a tray, allowing an observer to view the different sound waves. By building this speaker and observing the effects of energy on the sand, Julia examined the physics of sound waves while learning about science, art, and shop standards. Throughout the rest of the year, other students approached Julia directly to ask about music and music production, and she realized that she had the knowledge and the confidence to give advice. Julia attended the PBL school for three years. She had started behind in high school credits by a full year but, at the PBL school, she graduated on time and left high school having already lined up a series of gigs throughout the summer working alongside a professional DJ.

The staff focused on allowing Julia to complete something they knew she could and would do really well. Sometimes people need to be allowed to do what they love in order to empower them to want to learn.

Questions that we found useful to ask ourselves during this project were:

- How do you identify the individual needs of your learners?
- How do you serve them?
- How do you facilitate the transition to project-based learning?

Transitioning to the PBL Environment

In a traditional school, the focus is on standardization and equality. In a project-based environment, we focus on the individual learning process and equity. That is, we approach each learner as unique. Learners are not all painted with the same brush. Individual learning plans are created for each learner and success means different things to each learner, relative to the realities of their lives. We meet the students where they are and collaborate with them to create and adapt a learning system that works for them. This transition involves a significant upfront investment of time and energy, but the reward can be phenomenal. It is often a bumpy road, and requires support and encouragement for both the learner and the educator. This process will be different for each educator and each student, but it can be helpful to keep the following in mind:

- **Change is hard.** As educators, we sometimes revert to the education style that we encountered as students. Take a step back. Learning from the past is a good thing, but recreating it is not our goal. We are asking the learners to undergo a complete change in perspective, thought process, and function. This experience will be easier for some than for others, but it will undoubtedly take time.
- **Relationships matter.** Project-based learning relies heavily on strong, healthy relationships. Take the time to get to know your students as people. The transition to project-based learning will be smoother and, ultimately, faster if you are able to support your students by genuinely knowing them and encouraging them to pursue meaningful projects.

1,000 Ways to Die: A Life-Science Course

Science is arguably one of the easier subjects for teachers to create projects in and around. Scientific experimentation is a form of project-based learning that traditional schools have embraced, familiar to many of us (educators) during our own school careers. 1,000 Ways to Die was a brainchild of two educators who wanted to take project-based science to the next level. This six-week course engaged first-aid training as the primary vehicle for teaching life sciences.

We (the staff) set ourselves a challenge. We weren't going to focus solely on the subject matter, but rather on scenarios and situations that contained the subject matter and were particularly relatable or relevant to the learners involved. In fact, we used the course as a litmus test, asking ourselves, "As teachers, do we really need to have people fill in a diagram of a body system, or can students learn all of that information better on their own, and in relation to their own interests, given the right situation?" We also wanted students to walk away with relevant life skills: first-aid knowledge and training, awareness of the impact of drinking and drugs on driving, safety in the home and workplace, and fire safety. We challenged ourselves to create a course that was adaptive, fully engaging, and fun. The result was an environment where students *chose* to engage with science because of their own curiosity.

Each week involved a different situation. For example, the first week was based around the broad question: "What is death?" This is a brutal subject, but the students reacted well to honest discussion around mortality, leading us into conversation of scientific and spiritual topics. From a purely physiologic point of view, death is simply when the body stops functioning. Students wanted to know, "What is death?" "Why does the body die if the heart stops beating?" "How is everything connected?" Their curiosity led them to ask for a basic introduction to body systems – functions, effects, and interdependency. Although the subject was life science, learners were really delving into developing skills in inquiry and problem solving.

Generally, half of each week was focused on problem and inquiry-based learning about the body systems, often self-led, either individually or in groups, depending on the student. We would start a lesson with a situation: you've cut your arm, and it's bleeding a lot. Then we opened the floor to questions, prompting when necessary. How do I deal with a bleeding wound? How much blood is there in the body? How much blood can the body lose before systems start to fail? Why does the body need blood? What's in blood? What kind of diseases can be transmitted in blood? The students ultimately discovered and shared the answers to all of their questions.

The other part of each week involved first-aid scenarios focused on the skills and learning related to the specific body system or the questions that students had asked during class. The first week, we learned how to measure the body's vital signs, leading us to question what normal vitals were, what abnormal signs signified, and how to address them. In later weeks, we engaged in full-blown scenarios, complete with moulage (mock injuries made using make-up and a variety of other ingredients), where students acted as first responders to the scene of an injury and used their skills, knowledge, and judgment to solve the problems they were confronted with.

The challenge for us as educators was trying to quantify the scientific knowledge that students gained throughout the program. We intentionally didn't use worksheets or exams because we believe that skills and experience take priority over learning by rote. We had to trust in the process and continually remind ourselves that it was happening. The students' actions, decisions, and behaviour during those scenarios showed that they had discovered important connections between their knowledge of anatomy and biology and the hard skills of first-aid training. We didn't tell them, or teach them, these connections. They discovered the connections through inquiry and experience.

Often, our class discussions and individual student conversations moved beyond what students were learning to *why* they wanted to learn about the subject and *how* they were actually learning. We would inquire, "What made you want to ask that question?" "Who's talking the most here?" "How is what you are engaged in working for you?" We pushed the students to examine their softer skills and then make intentional adjustments as they progressed in the class. For example, students who were always taking the lead in scenarios were encouraged to allow someone else to step forward and then observe the differences in leadership styles between others and themselves, analyzing how different styles work in different settings and identifying areas for their personal improvement.

We had initially set out to run a class that covered anatomy and body systems, drawing on our first aid/medical backgrounds as wilderness first responders and emergency medical technicians, but it turned out to be more than that. We let curiosity reign, and saw that innovation and problem solving naturally followed. We observed that students identified unique and important problems without being told what to look for; they asked in-depth questions from a wide range of angles and utilized their existing skills and knowledge to build new learning methodologies and come up with ideas for solving the identified problems.

This approach does not reflect the traditional model of high school. Not all of our students ended the term being able to name every part of the circulatory system, but that is okay because they know what the heart does and what happens if it stops. They know and have hands-on experience with different ways of addressing, and sometimes solving, common injuries and medical problems. Ultimately, they showed us that when given the opportunity to be curious and explore new terrain, they were able to ask the questions that helped them find the answers that they were seeking.

Questions that we found useful to ask ourselves during this project were:

- How do you encourage curiosity?
- How might you measure the whole student's progress?
- How do you balance the time between academic pursuits and the social and emotional development of learners?
- What is the next challenge that you will set yourself as an educator?

Development of the Whole Learner

In the project-based environment, we strive to recognize the learner as a whole person. We focus on the relevant skills and knowledge that learners will need to be successful in their lives. In addition, we often rely on tools like Maslow's hierarchy to identify areas of improvement. We tailor our support, from the challenges that we help create to the style of communication that we use to build rapport, to the apparent needs of each individual. We recognize that success may look different from student to student, and that we cannot dictate what it means. It can be helpful to consider that:

- **Failure is an iteration of success.** As humans, we have a tendency to be critical. Whether we've perceived our own failure, or the failure of others,

this perception tends to cloud our judgment and affect our behaviour. Project-based learning encourages students to try, regardless of the likelihood of success. This process is a useful tool for identifying areas of improvement, and learning to "fail" is an invaluable skill for achieving success in life.
- **Success does not have a norm.** Our students are individuals. They have unique experiences, backgrounds, beliefs, and situations. Their starting point will be unique as well, and we are in no way endowed with any magical ability to know where they will end up. That said, we can still create an environment in which they can dream, plan, and experiment. We can trust them to find their own greatness, and respect what success means to them.

→ Don't agree; there are common elements of being successful (effort, engagement)

Building Wolf Boxes

Last year, the local wildlife centre contacted one of our schools to see if we could help build new wolf boxes (doghouses for wolves). This could have been a great stand-alone project for one student or a group of students, but we decided to use the project to help a particular group of students develop the socio-emotional skills in their own "toolboxes."

The group was handpicked by several staff members with the intention of including students whose strengths lay in hands-on projects, but who could benefit from focused improvement in social and emotional skills. We focused on team power, selecting students who struggled in social settings, particularly those who had difficulty feeling that they belonged. The six students were all very different and from different social groups. Normally, they would not be seen socializing together. The big challenge for the students in this group was exactly that – working in a group. They were all very used to doing their own thing.

This was a real project. It was not engineered by an educator or controlled within the confines of the school. The students worked directly with one teacher and with the professional staff at the wildlife centre. The team met every morning to work for one-and-a-half to two hours. They figured out what information they needed and worked with the teacher to think through how to approach the wildlife centre staff and ask their questions. They went out to the centre and met the staff to gather the information. They identified what needed to be built, exploring the requirements of the wolves as well as those of the staff through inquiry, research, and discussion. They took these factors and developed a physical design, using it to decide what materials were required and how many boxes they would need to build. These tasks required that they not only work together as a team, but also establish a rapport with working adults. They then had to figure out who was going to do what, and how to move forward as a group with the project.

In school, at the start of this project, it looked like one teacher managing six individual students. There didn't appear to be very much collaboration or teamwork amongst the students. The teacher walked the group through the first box, showing them how to build it. The group was then tasked with building the remaining three boxes. As the weeks went on, the learners started to manage each other. They began to hold each other accountable, giving each other direct feedback when people went off task or failed to pull their weight. They were able to cooperatively agree about when and how to redirect efforts in the pursuit of common priorities.

The project started off as "we're helping the teacher make these boxes." By the end of the term, it was "look what we've built!" During the project, we began to see the same progression mirrored in the students' other classes. They held themselves more accountable for their progress and behaviour outside of the wolf box project.

For example, Jimmy knew that his phone was a distraction for him. He decided to start handing it in. He would set himself a work schedule where he would focus on a project or assignment for a set amount of time, allow himself a phone break, and then continue working. He developed this strategy in the mornings, during the wolf box project, after other students gave him feedback on overuse of his phone. He carried this strategy over to his afternoon classes without prompting.

Sarah knew that she learned better when she was moving around, so she started advocating in other classes for freedom to move. She asked teachers to let her know when she could move, saying that movement helped her process information. When a teacher gave her the green light, she would pace in a designated area for the allotted amount of time. Her work output increased dramatically, her behaviour issues decreased, and she gained confidence and self-awareness through advocating for her needs and finding solutions that worked for the group.

It was also clear that new friendships had formed as a result of the project. As these six students passed each other during the day, they would acknowledge and greet each other. This built bridges between different friendship circles within the school. Tools for success have the capacity to go far beyond what we traditionally view as academic skills in scope, breadth, and depth.

Questions that we found useful to ask ourselves during this project were:

- What tools do you feel are necessary for success in life?
- How do you identify each individual student's tools and their effectiveness?
- How can you structure classes to include toolbox development?
- When did you last sharpen your own tools?

→ Connects to Tao & finding strengths

Building the Student Toolbox

Whether it is a product of nature or nurture, or a combination of both, each person is equipped with a unique toolbox – a set of skills for personal, socio-emotional, academic, and extracurricular success that is specific to each individual's personality, disposition, and goals. Some of us are great at networking; others can rally the support of people; others can capture complex emotions in the stroke of a paintbrush; the list goes on. This diversity is what makes humankind so vibrant and unique. In the project-based environment, we have the opportunity to help our students identify which tools they have in their toolboxes, which are missing, and which need sharpening. While students will ultimately need a unique set of tools that suits their life, profession, and personality, there are some standard items that come in handy for all of us. When developing these social and emotional tools, we have found it helpful to remember that:

- **Admitting weakness is hard.** Each of us has skills that can be improved, and sometimes it's hard to admit this to others, and harder still to actively do something about it. Yet, this is precisely what is expected of learners (and educators!) in the PBL environment. Sometimes it can help to show others that we aren't perfect, either. We are real people who make mistakes and work hard to do our best.

- **You know yourself better than anyone.** No matter how tempting it is to think that we have great ideas or have dealt with a similar situation in the past, we ultimately don't know what is best for our students. They know themselves better than we ever will, and they'll know how to best help themselves. Our experience and advice can be helpful, but such ideas are better used as resources to help our students find their own solutions.

Conclusion

Transitioning to project-based learning is not easy. It requires commitment from learners and educators to think creatively in order to overcome the unique challenges that each individual will face. It also requires that people orient themselves within a new system of education that recognizes and adapts for each individual, a system where there is rarely, if ever, a norm.

There isn't one right way of doing project-based learning. It will, and should, look different from student to student, between educators, and from school to school, based on the individuals involved. And, it is not simply a methodology within the confines of the classroom. Project-based learning is a process. It helps develop an environment, a culture, and also a community. It facilitates a gradual but pervasive change in perspectives and attitudes. PBL is about what happens outside of the projects and the school just as much as it is about what happens in the "classroom." This approach gives freedom and flexibility to both learners and educators so they can create a healthy learning environment for themselves. It values and supports the whole student, empowering learners to focus on their interests and discover relevant connections between their lives and their schooling.

This process can be complex, but there are key factors in common across environments. In our experience, we've found that a focus on the whole learner, with particular attention to socio-emotional skills, not only makes the transition to PBL smoother, but also positively affects academic performance and personal development. As educators, we challenge ourselves to help learners develop the knowledge and skills that they need to thrive in life. This approach means being real with our students and creating an environment where they can be real with us. We take the time to know who our students are as whole individuals so that we can work with them on projects that actually mean something to them. We learn our students' names and appreciate their personalities; we listen to their struggles and successes; we try to understand their lives in and outside of school; and we put ourselves in their shoes in order to support them to the best of our ability. We take the time to hear about a learner's argument with their sibling. We check in to understand what meals, if any, each learner has been eating. We pay attention to their behaviour and appearance, observing to check that they are well-rested and engaged.

We process this information to better position ourselves to support our learners, regardless of whether this support is solely academic or personal. This attention might mean taking time from academic pursuits to address deeper issues with learners. We find that spending such meaningful time has a great deal of impact on their progress, empowering learners to apply their skills and interests more constructively. We create space for our students to be human, and also let others see our human side – that we too make mistakes but are constantly working hard to improve. We learn what fires up our students, what challenges them, and where their comfort zones reside. We actively show them that we care and adapt our support to fit each individual's needs. We support them through success and through iterations of success, even when that success looks unfamiliar to us. We hold ourselves to the same expectations that we do our students.

References

Adkins, A. (2016, May 12). Millennials: The job-hopping generation. *Gallup.* Retrieved from www.gallup.com/businessjournal/191459/millennials-job-hopping-generation.aspx

Dishman, L. (2016, May 24). These are the biggest skills that new graduates lack. *Fast Company.* Retrieved from www.fastcompany.com/3059940/the-future-of-work/these-are-the-biggest-skills-that-new-graduates-lack

Kolb, D.A. (1984). *Experiential learning: Experience as the source of learning and development.* Prentice-Hall Inc.

Maslow, A.H. (1943). A theory of human motivation. *Psychological Review, 50* (4), 430-437.

About the Author

Dave Law has taught in alternative education settings for 13 years, first as a teacher at Eagles' Circle School – an off-campus program for at-risk middle years students – and then for 11 years at Churchill High School in the Grades 7–8 Flexible Learning program. He currently teaches Grade 11 at the Seven Oaks Met School. Dave has presented on inquiry-based learning in Denver and Chicago for the Coalition of Essential Schools and was the keynote speaker – along with four of his students – at the 2017 Spring Forum of the Manitoba Education Research Network (MERN). His master's thesis on inquiry-based learning and mathematics was published as a part of MERN's second monograph series.

Who Should Read This Chapter?

Teacher candidates and teachers interested in PBL, thematic projects, and/or inquiry-based learning.

The Theme of This Chapter in Three Words

Curriculum into projects.

As an Educator, What Are You Passionate About?

I'm passionate about creating a culture in my classroom and in my school where students feel they're an active part of their own education. I'm passionate about learning and about witnessing the spark of discovery in my students that drives learning. I strive to foster a classroom where authentic learning occurs and to create an understanding among my students that I'm a fellow learner who is interested in exploring the truth of our world along with them.

CHAPTER 3

How Can Teachers Engage Students with Specific Learning Outcomes (SLOs) While Still Remaining True to the Spirit of Inquiry?

Dave Law, Seven Oaks Met School
Winnipeg, Manitoba, Canada

Forging ahead with large-scale inquiry-based projects can be exhilarating and exciting, but also terrifying. What will our theme be? Will the students be interested in this theme? How can I involve them in a meaningful way? Yes, it's "about the process," but what if the process is a disaster?

I've been facilitating and co-facilitating massive cross-curricular projects in the Grades 7 and 8 Flexible Learning ("Flex") program at Churchill High School – a multi-age program with a focus on inquiry-based learning – for over ten years. A concern about these projects that has continually been raised is how to connect our endeavours to the curriculum in a meaningful way.

As teachers, we want our students – sometimes above all else – to be engaged. If we operated along the lines of true inquiry (i.e., not prescribing a teacher-talky list of steps but allowing kids to study whatever they're interested in), students would be able to work on almost anything they wanted to. Although the Flex program allowed this kind of inquiry to transpire (maker spaces, for example), the instances were few and far between. The majority of our projects, especially the bigger, long-term ones, were beholden to the outcomes of the four core subjects that we taught. But what if students have no prior knowledge of the particle theory? What if they haven't done any projects in

English in the past? What if, most importantly, they have no interest in learning about ancient societies, optics, or patterns and relations?

In this chapter, I will outline an activity called "Plan Our Year," which addressed the need to connect our projects to the curriculum in a meaningful way. Through this activity, we realized that other concerns were addressed as well. By connecting authentically with the curriculum, we found that the theme essentially chose itself, our students became more involved in their experience, and engagement improved immensely. We realized that the curriculum is an important guide, but that it should be used merely as a starting point. As long as our projects allowed for a significant amount of freedom for students to take their learning in any direction they chose, they were able to achieve incredible things that went above and beyond the original curricular outcomes.

→ Post exhibition strat.

Plan Our Year

Soon after we were hired as teachers in the Flex program, my teaching partner and I identified the disparity between projects and outcomes as something we wanted to address head-on. Years earlier, we had worked at an arts camp where we had great success outlining to students the possibilities in drama, music, and art before they decided on which of these three paths to follow. Wanting to emulate that experience, we brainstormed ways in which we could lay out all the possibilities of the grades 7 and 8 curricula for our students. What we ended up with was an activity that we named "Plan Our Year."

Step 1: Gathering the Class

We designed this activity to make students feel empowered and excited about middle years – no small feat – and we made sure to start it before the end of the first week of school so they would go home on their first weekend with excitement. This timing also ensured we would have momentum going into the second week. We began by bringing together all the students in the program – approximately 60 grades 7 and 8 students in one classroom. My teaching partner began with an emphatic speech about the importance of including things we were passionate about in our daily school work, and I tried my best shot at an inspiring speech about their unique opportunity to direct what they were to learn during the upcoming year. Then we sent our students home

CHAPTER 3   31

with a homework assignment: Talk to your parents and ask them to help you brainstorm at least five projects you would love to do this year at school.

On the Monday of the second week, we gathered the students again and asked a few to informally share their homework assignment. Beforehand, we made sure to instill our maxim in them: "No judgment in brainstorming." We listened to their ideas and validated them, no matter how outlandish they were.

At this point, we took some time to teach our students about the curriculum by asking them questions and fielding responses. Why do schools teach the things they do? Who tells schools what to teach? What does *curriculum* even mean? What does the term *outcome* refer to? We showed the class a couple of curriculum documents on the projector screen and we viewed several specific learning outcomes from a number of subject areas. We explained that, as a class, we would be studying these outcomes and would use them to plan the majority of projects and assignments we would embark upon during the upcoming school year.

Step 2: Favourite-Subject Groupings

We then organized students into groups that represented their favourite core subjects (English, mathematics, social studies, and science). We limited the size of the groups to approximately 12 students, and reorganized on the fly. We had the social studies and English groups meet in my teaching partner's classroom, while the math and science groups met in my room. Next, we handed out the first of two rounds of graphic organizers, which asked students to brainstorm ideas for projects in their groups and write them down.

The next step was the most crucial one, and it is the step that we created to directly address the disparity between inquiry and the curriculum. A few days before the first day of school, my teaching partner and I acquired all of the specific learning outcomes for the four core subjects. Then we did our best to rewrite the curricular text in kid-friendly language. For example, "Locate on a map and describe the impact of the Viking invasions on Europe from the 9th to 12th centuries" became "Study the Vikings and map out their invasions" (Manitoba Education and Training, 2003). Next, we printed them off. Finally, we cut the list of outcomes into strips of paper and sorted them into manila envelopes based on which subject they corresponded with. When the students settled in their subject groups, we handed them the envelopes and asked them to take out outcomes at random and try to think of fun projects, assignments, or activities they could do that would address these outcomes. My teaching partner and I circulated and helped groups as needed.

Once most of the groups had generated at least three good ideas each, we reconvened as a whole Flex class the next period to share them. As the representatives from each group began to talk, we could already feel we were on to something. Some students were near breathless as they explained their ideas about a movie they could make for English, or a math assignment that would help them study area by designing their dream house. The social studies group talked about staging a medieval war and the science groups shared their eagerness to participate in certain labs or dissect certain body parts. When the lab discussion veered toward Frankenstein territory, we gently steered it back toward the curriculum, reminding them that the human body was part of it and that we could, for example, dissect a heart – although not a human one! Some students began to test our openness at this point, suggesting playing video games for an English project. Noting our "no judgment" mantra once again, we gave examples where video games could indeed meet the curriculum, such as storyboarding a game for English or studying the effects of gaming for a science project.

Step 3: Reverse Jigsaw

The next class, we prepared our students for the next phase of the Plan Our Year activity by defining the term *integration* and explaining how most careers resist neat categorization into separate subjects. In fact, we challenged students to think of jobs that only use math skills or only use skills taught in English. After all, accountants need to write resumes and writers need to do their taxes. It did not take much to convince the students that learning subjects in isolation can be an inauthentic way of learning and does not accurately reflect how subjects are applied outside of school.

Once we had piqued their interest, we explained that, for the next step, students would be meeting in heterogeneous groups with representatives from all four core subjects. Once in these groups, we explained that we wanted them to come up with as many large-scale, integrated, cross-curricular projects as possible. We numbered students from one to four, had them meet in their number groups, and, once again, handed out worksheets so they could record their ideas. When we circulated, we encouraged them to think big and try to contribute their knowledge of their favourite subject from the previous class.

This part of the activity was inspired by the cooperative-learning strategy known as a jigsaw. (In a jigsaw activity, small groups of learners are tasked with researching, thinking about, and communicating a small body of knowledge that they can bring back to the larger group and share.)

Step 4: Whole-Class Brainstorming Session

Once these groups had generated a few ideas each, we congregated as a class for one last time. This brainstorming session went even better than before. Once one or two ideas had been put forward, the floodgates opened. Ideas built on ideas, some outlandish, but most not. All were, in the opinion of my teaching partner and me, better than anything we could have imagined. My teaching partner attempted to scrawl the students' ideas on the whiteboard while I fielded remarks, trying to keep students from excitedly talking over each other. Every speaker gushed with enthusiasm and eagerness about the possibilities. Ideas kept building on ideas, and I found myself joining the fray. "Yes, we could totally study Roman structures in science and then use that knowledge to make the classroom into ancient Rome!" "Could we make a Roman market?" "That's math, selling and buying stuff." "What about Egypt?" "We should have Egypt and Rome!" "Oh my gosh, we could have a trade war between two classes!" I felt flushed and beyond excited. I was in a state of flow and so were many of my students.

By the end of the brainstorming session, our whiteboard was filled with ideas. Arrows were drawn to connect related concepts and ideas were crammed into corners. As a class, we generated several really solid ideas for thematic projects as well as other great concepts for smaller in-class assignments. Even when the bell rang for lunch, several students – some of whom were too shy to share in front of the class – rushed toward us with more ideas. There was a buzz about the group and a shared sense of excitement about what we were about to embark upon. In the past, I'd occasionally created decent projects for my classes, and students had been excited when I presented my ideas to them. However, what I experienced after that first brainstorming session eclipsed all of my past successes. Not only were the ideas we generated much better than anything I could have come up with, but the students demonstrated an exponentially higher level of enthusiasm than anything I'd observed before. That enthusiasm was infectious, and my teaching partner and I felt a renewed sense of purpose to make our students' ideas come to fruition.

This activity was obviously hugely successful and resulted in our first multi-week, integrated project.

Try it out next year.

Egypt and Rome

In Manitoba, the grade 8 social-studies curriculum is about world history. The first cluster of outcomes concern ancient societies, and these outcomes were the focus of the first project that we put into action from our Plan Our Year activity. We decided to focus on an Egypt and Rome theme and made a plan to transform our classrooms into these respective societies.

It worked out that a majority of female students wanted to study Rome and a majority of male students wanted to study Egypt, and they voted overwhelmingly to split the class along gender lines. At the time, my teaching partner and I were reluctant to split the class this way. Indeed, this is something we would never consider nowadays, as both of us are much more educated on the issues surrounding sexuality and gender. However, we were determined to allow our students to have a true democratic voice, so we went ahead with their idea.

We decided to wait until mid-November to start what turned into a massive project spanning two classrooms. The wait was due to the need for a firm deadline (i.e., the winter break) as well as for time to set class expectations and to scaffold new grade 7 students into the routines of middle school. My classroom became "Ancient Egypt" and my teaching partner's became "Ancient Rome."

Our students split into groups of their choice of two to five, while a few operated individually. To incorporate English outcomes into the project, we included a written research piece. Each member of each group had to provide research on five aspects of their ancient society in the form of paragraphs. It was important for us to make sure each student had a separate part of the project that they had to work on individually. The reason for this was twofold. First, the individual component helped to keep certain students in certain groups from doing the majority of the work. Second, many of our students came from non-alternative programs in their elementary schools and were overwhelmed at the scale of the project and its openness. The research piece was meant to be fairly concrete to allow these students to scaffold up to the project's open-ended hands-on component.

The second component for each group was to collaboratively contribute a tangible piece of work that represented either Rome or Egypt. This component also met curricular skills in social studies and English that required students to work together to create an artifact of learning (Manitoba Education and Training, 1996, 2003). One example of this component was a desk-sized model of the Sphinx that one group designed and created. Another group built a model of the Roman Colosseum. One group of boys were not interested in anything hands-on, and so I helped them write and film a movie about a group of tomb raiders. Another student created a Roman mural.

Within a few days, two-thirds of the Roman class decided to collectively create an ancient Roman market, complete with booths, music, and wares, which included handmade jewelry, clothing, and weapons.

The entire process was messy, exhausting, exhilarating, and, in the end, an overall success. Our classrooms looked fantastic, and we invited some of the high-school classes as well as our administrators to view our work and peruse the Roman market. Shortly after, we brought our students' parents in for a potluck one evening to show off the work and get to know each other.

However, there were many challenges that we had not foreseen. The entire process took about five weeks, but it was clear that we had started too late. Throughout the last week, my teaching partner and I, along with several students and a teacher candidate, were putting in long hours at lunch and after school frantically trying to finish the project before the winter break. The process was also very noisy and messy. We annoyed some of the other teachers and custodial staff, and feedback from many of our students suggested that it was difficult to operate in the chaotic classroom environment.

There are many examples of the kind of chaos that occurred during the Egypt and Rome project. Early on, a few boys and girls collaborated to set up a pulley system between our two classrooms. At first, they were sending witty and interesting letters to each other in the style of ancient citizens. The boys sent notes in hieroglyphs and the girls translated them and sent back messages in Latin. However, without direct supervision, this exercise quickly devolved into notes on any subject different from the topic at hand. Some notes became threatening and/or inappropriate, and friendly competition between the two classes quickly got out of hand. Within a day or two, we had to put a stop to the pulley letters, and we had a class discussion about competition versus collaboration.

Another source of problems was the infamous River Nile in my classroom, which was created to incorporate the outcome, "Give examples of the influence of the natural environment on ways of life in an early society of Mesopotamia, Egypt, or the Indus Valley." A large group of students wanted to build a huge model of the Nile that would have running water. None of us had any idea about how to create this, but we went ahead without a coherent plan. The model ended up being about a metre wide and spanning the entire width of my classroom, which caused problems when I had to teach other classes like Math and Health in the same room. In these classes, we had to rearrange the desks every period and students had to jump over the river to get to the other side of the room. When it was mostly finished, we decided to spray paint it outside. It took the entire class to carry it outside, like a giant anaconda. We happened to do this on a particularly windy Manitoba day, and the moment we set it down it blew apart into a thousand pieces.

There was one major concern. Though the project was an overall hit and included some phenomenal work, a few students had very little to show after four weeks. One student ended up submitting absolutely nothing. My teaching partner and I found ourselves extremely busy during the project, and it was relatively easy for a few kids to "fly under the radar" and avoid work. We felt we did not do enough to engage these students and to make them more accountable.

Nevertheless, the project was an overall success, and most of the feedback from students, parents, and staff was very positive. It was a huge learning experience for the students as well as the teachers.

The Sustainable City

One of our more recent and successful projects was our "Sustainable City." It also demonstrated how my teaching partner and I learned from our previous successes and failures. This project focused on a different group of outcomes from the grade 7 social studies curriculum: about human impact on the environment and how that affects society (Manitoba Education and Training, 2003). We also included a number of grade 7 science outcomes from the "Interactions with Ecosystems" unit, which has components that address the impact of human activity on the natural environment (Manitoba Education and Training, 2000).

The physical project was even larger in scale than Egypt and Rome because we had moved to a different part of the school where three classrooms were joined together and separated by folding walls. The middle room became our workspace, where the model city we ended up building took up the entire classroom from end to end and floor to ceiling.

We limited groups to pairs. Each group had to create a to-scale neighbourhood of their design, which included their own residence. These neighbourhoods, made out of recycled cardboard with repurposed science-fair backboards as bases, were attached at the end of the project and arranged around a downtown area, full of model towers that each group was required to design and build. Both the neighbourhoods and the towers had to include five sustainable technologies, which groups had to write about in accompanying research booklets.

Student-built neighbourhoods, Sustainable City project.

While working on this project and others, we learned to lessen the chaos by carefully building up to the project over the first few weeks. To address the science curriculum's focus on the principles of sustainable development, we brought in a prominent architect to discuss sustainable design and how to create walkable, people-friendly neighbourhoods. We invited a pair of local urban farmers to talk to our class about sustainable agricultural practices. My teaching partner addressed some Indigenous perspectives in her English classes, and I discussed human impact on the environment in social studies. By the time we actually started the project, students had a well of information they could apply to their particular projects.

Another strategy we began to use in our Flex program to create some accountability was instructing students to complete a smaller component in their projects before they could move on to a larger one. In an ancient-societies-themed project like Egypt and Rome, this component could be a small artifact – like a dagger or a piece of jewelry – that they had to create and hand in for marks before they could move on, say, to building a structure or filming a movie. In our Sustainable City project, this smaller component took the form of their personal

> use traffic stop to scaffold

residence, which we called their "Dream House." Knowing that this was going to be an important tool for scaffolding, I made sure we prioritized learning about scale, area, and other spatial topics in my math class.

By the time we began the Sustainable City, students had a significant knowledge base of green technology and architecture, and so some groups went the extra mile by incorporating futuristic technologies. For example, one group studied a technology in which an enormous satellite collects solar energy in outer space and beams it down to Earth.

Students also became heavily invested in making sure the Sustainable City was as environmentally sustainable as possible. Students could only use recycled or repurposed materials for their projects. All of the cardboard used was scavenged from recycling bins and old science fair backboards. Once we knew that we wanted to have lighting, one student volunteered to transform an old bicycle into a pedal-powered producer of electricity (right).

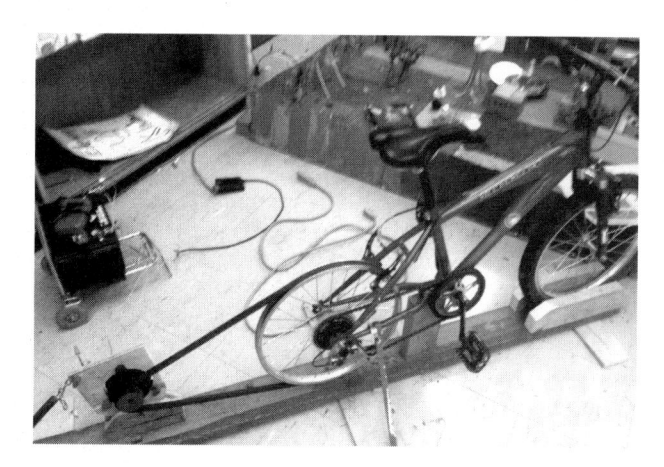

As with the Egypt and Rome project, my teaching partner and I received a great deal of positive feedback from students, parents, and staff. We even received some media attention from a couple of local news outlets. There was, however, one major difference from the Egypt and Rome project. This time, we received virtually no negative feedback and felt that the project was hugely successful. We especially felt that this project successfully balanced student interest with new, profound learning. The fact that we also met a massive number of curricular outcomes was a bonus.

Plan Our Year Today

Over the next decade, we continued to use the Plan Our Year activity every year. Although it remained mostly the same, we instituted some tweaks along the way.

Originally, we planned to have four large groups that corresponded to the four core subjects. However, over the years we have worked to break up the larger groups into smaller units of six to eight students. In our program, because we've known the grade 8s for a whole year, we can quickly eyeball which ones will work well together and take on leadership roles in their groups. The grade 7s are still in a state of shock about the new school year, and we count on the grade 8s to guide them through the Plan Our Year process.

The social state of some of these students is also why we keep the groups as large as we do. Inevitably, there are grade 7s who are overwhelmed and shy, and we want them to feel safe and not too pressured to get involved in the activity. What we have observed is that the introverted students tend to observe the process while it is occurring, and then approach us later to share their ideas.

Another reason to be open to different-sized groups is that there tends to be a preference for certain subjects. English, for instance, tends to be a popular subject, while often math is (tragically) the students' least favourite subject. In our program, I spend the most time facilitating the math group, as it's challenging for most students to translate the SLOs into actual assignments and projects.

Over the years, the teachers in the program have been forced to adapt to many changes in enrolment. The number of students in our program has fluctuated wildly, from less than 40 grades 7 and 8 students to 75. In the years with higher enrolment, we met in the school's multi-purpose room. For two of those years, our school hired a third teacher and created a third class to accommodate the extra people. With three full classes operating on the same projects, we had to be extremely creative in order to make everything we wanted to do possible.

Assessment

Based on years of facilitating large-scale thematic projects, our assessment has remained fairly constant. Before we begin a project, we bring the students together as a group and brainstorm what the project will look like and how it will be assessed. Students and teachers collaborate to create a rubric, and the teacher negotiates the values that are attributed to each aspect of the rubric. Since we began starting with a small artifact/component first, we make a separate, simple rubric for that as well (see example opposite).

We also always include a self-assessment at the end of the project and make this part of their final mark. We have found that, generally speaking, students are much harder on themselves than we would be, so we make this part of the assessment less than 20% of their overall mark. On these self-assessments, we always leave room for reflection – "If you were to engage in this kind of project again, what would you do differently?" – as well as general comments.

Name: _____   Date: _____

ANCIENT SOCIETIES ARTIFACT PROJECT

What ancient society did you choose? _____

ARTIFACT:

Create an artifact that relates to your ancient society and discuss what the artifact was and how it was used. This artifact could be any piece of this ancient society that one might find in a museum. Examples: a drawing/painting of hieroglyphics, religious art, Roman dagger, canopic jars, papyrus scroll, Roman coins, mummified skull, jewelry, tools, an ankh, flag, etc.

RUBRIC

Artifact (Did you attempt to be creative? Does it show? Did you put in a great deal of effort? Does your artifact resemble the image from your research?)
……………………………………………………………….. /5

Research: (Is your information correct? Did you answer the Five W's and H? Does it show that you have learned? Is there a picture included?)
……………………………………………………………….. /5

TOTAL

___/10

Due Date: Tuesday, Nov 29.

Lessons Learned

When I was studying to be a teacher, most of my professors made it very clear that the curriculum was of the utmost importance. In my program, we had several courses that were specifically designed to familiarize education students with the curricular outcomes of the core subjects. Once I had my own classroom, it was natural for me to focus on covering the curriculum.

Based on my post-secondary experiences regarding curriculum, especially near the end of the first Egypt and Rome project, I was extremely anxious about not meeting specific learning outcomes. I recall reading the Manitoba Social Studies Curricular Framework of Outcomes (2003) at the time to check up on what outcomes we had met so far and becoming highly stressed that I was not meeting every single one.

I went down to speak to the school's principal about my concerns about not meeting every outcome and my worries that this big project we had created was ruining my students' understanding of ancient societies. He smiled and calmly asked me what I remembered about my grade 8 social-studies experience. I told him, "Not much." But I did remember a project I worked on with my friend, and how we'd built a model castle. He told me that my 12- and 13-year-old students would remember almost no facts or dates, but they would remember this experience, and when they were older, they could look back and think, "That was so fun. History is cool." For my principal, it was more important that I was helping to create authentic learning experiences for my students, and that the curriculum should be used as a guide rather than a manual.

What is really great is that I've kept in touch with some of my former students and have been able to talk to them about our first big project, and my principal's predictions have absolutely come true. When I talk to those students today, they say things like, "That was the most fun I ever had in school," and "That was really crazy, but in a really good way." They can remember many specific instances from the project – such as the Nile incident – and they treasure those experiences. Their memories would not have been as vivid if I had chosen to study ancient societies through note-taking and tests.

These large projects and the Plan Our Year activity that led to them are great ways to connect curriculum to students in an authentic way. They show that it's important not to get bogged down in the details, and it's okay for learning to go in directions that are not necessarily a connection to the curriculum.

For instance, it would be a stretch to try to connect futuristic sustainable technologies like space solar panels to Manitoba's grade 7 science curriculum. However, they were absolutely learning about *science*. They were following their interests and taking their learning beyond the basics of the curriculum.

Taking students beyond the curriculum is the ultimate goal of education. Curriculum is important as a guide, but it might be better used as a starting point. The inquiry-based projects I have outlined have worked well for me to integrate curriculum while providing opportunities for students to go way beyond the baseline of what they "should" achieve. Whatever framework teachers choose to use – whether it's project-based learning, inquiry, direct teaching, or whatever – it is paramount that students have the ability to veer outside the boundaries of curricular outcomes and follow their own interests and passions.

References

Law, D. (1996). *K-8 English language arts: Manitoba curriculum framework of outcomes*. Winnipeg, MB: Manitoba Education and Training.

Law, D. (2000). *Grades 5 to 8 science: Manitoba curriculum framework of outcomes*. Winnipeg, MB: Manitoba Education and Training.

Law, D. (2003). *Kindergarten to grade 8 social studies: Manitoba curriculum framework of outcomes*. Winnipeg, MB: Manitoba Education and Training.

About the Author
Glenys MacLeod is a wife, and mother to two children. She is currently the vice-principal at École South Pointe School, a dual track kindergarten to grade 8 school in Winnipeg. She is also a graduate student at the University of Manitoba. Glenys is passionate about empowering students to be passionately curious, fearless in exploration, and relentless learners for life.

Who Should Read This Chapter?
This chapter is for mathematics educators and learners who are curious about making space for all kinds of ways to know and do math. It is for educators and learners who believe math can be full of new discoveries and possibilities.

The Theme of This Chapter in Three Words
Adventure, empowerment, possibilities.

As an Educator, What Are You Passionate About?
Learning.

CHAPTER 4
What Can We Learn When We Live the Math?

Glenys MacLeod, École South Pointe School
Winnipeg, Manitoba, Canada

To take on the challenges of the 21st century (Wagner and Dintersmith, 2015), we will all need to be more than just literate and numerate; we will need to be passionately curious, fearless in exploration, and relentless learners for life. Expeditionary learning (MacLeod, 2016) seeks to inspire a spirit of wonder and curiosity that stays with each learner for life.

With the turn of the millennium and the promise of change in education (Hayes Jacobs, 2010, Gardner, 2008, Dufour & Dufour, 2010), I imagined that student curiosity would take over in our schools and that students would become passionate explorers, intent on creating positive changes in the world through innovation and invention. I hoped that, as result of working collaboratively with others in creativity-intense environments, students would develop rich mathematical minds along with the confidence to seek out and ask authentic questions, to investigate unknowns, and to embrace uncertainty as an endless potential for learning. I dreamt of exploring local communities in search of meaningful problems that would require my students and me to draw upon a variety of flexible, nonstandard problem-solving strategies. I imagined that schools would now "place in students' hands the exhilarating power to follow trails of interest, to make connections, to reformulate ideas, and to reach unique conclusions" (Brooks & Brooks, 1999, p. 22). I saw every space as a learning place, and all people and all things as teachers.

Bringing this vision of learning to life has been a challenge. Along the way, I've come to know with certainty that shared experience brings shared understanding, that knowledge is not a commodity but a continuous event, that learning is best when flexible and that content is richest when it is unbounded.

Living these beliefs has allowed for the creation of a project-based, expeditionary learning model for teaching mathematics (MacLeod, 2016). Expeditionary mathematics is learned by being in the field, where mathematicians do their learning and work, and by retelling the stories of our adventures.

Expeditionary Math

An expedition begins when students explore their community. When learning reaches from the classroom into the community, students build connections between theory and practice, concept and process, and content and context. In sharp contrast to a field trip, a learning expedition requires students to become a part of an uncertain and problematic situation. This experience of "learning at the edge means challenging old boundaries between school and community, between academic subjects and real-world problems, between theory and action, between thinking and doing" (Boss, 2012, p. 123).

Through these lived expeditionary experiences, learners shape their own ways of knowing and thinking about their world, their own approaches to solving problems, and their own learning processes. To be actively learning means to be fully engaged in an ongoing cycle of wondering, exploring, researching, developing, creating, constructing, connecting, communicating, reasoning, and reflecting. These skills are best developed out in our communities because deep thinking "cannot be removed from the world in which we live" (Roberts, 2012, p. 51). By extending our learning in all directions, all learners are welcomed with accessible content, a range of actions, and endless possible paths. It is only when lived personal experience and theoretical content are tied together that a greater understanding of the world begins to take shape. This learning "on location" encourages participation in local and global events beyond the school day, as learners become deeply involved in the exploration of their connection with their own community.

A student's approach to learning should be personally defined over time through experiences in a variety of learning environments. Students come to recognize which strategies are best suited for themselves as learners and best suited to the task at hand.

Workshops, Fieldwork, Mini-lessons, and Conferences

The learning community must be a dynamic, flexible, and vibrant space. Decisions about the academic content to be explored, resources to be used, and the assessment data to be gathered are made with the students, during the learning, and vary depending upon the ever-evolving path of each learner. To achieve this dynamic mix of teaching and learning strategies from workshops to mini-lessons and conferences to fieldwork invites all learners into an inclusive environment where opportunities exist for learning at multiple levels.

A linear curricular plan is difficult to draw for this model of learning as its path is always in motion. Instead, a curricular map is used so that the mathematical content, skills, behaviours, and attitudes blend and can be presented concurrently. The map also lends itself to the more cyclical nature of learning in which students cycle through stages of concrete experimentation, reflective observation, conceptualization, and active experimentation. Each learner enters into an adventure at their own entry point, and it is their own observations that develop into their own questions for experimentation.

Workshops

A workshop is a lively exchange of ideas. The purpose of the workshop varies according to the immediate needs of the students. Workshops may be discussions, spirited debates, planning sessions, or times to calculate, build models, experiment, or share results.

A workshop group.

Students may work in small collaborative groups or individually. It is not intended that all students take part in the same activity at the same time. These workshops encourage exchanges between learners where new discoveries can be verified and new understandings shared. When a team makes a new discovery, such as a strategy, connection, or conclusion that would be beneficial for others to know, educators send other students over to consult or bring everyone together for a few minutes to learn from that team. Through sharing what they have tried and learned, students become learning resources for each other.

Workshops provide extensive opportunities for social inclusion. As defined by Katz (2013), social inclusion means that "all students have opportunities to be part of the school community and to learn alongside their peers" (p. 11). To be socially included means to have a "sense of belonging and connectedness" (Katz, 2013, p. 11). Workshops are fluid and grow from the inquiry questions and plans of so many students, allowing them to branch out in many different ways. The workshop is significantly different from a traditional classroom in that student interactions are constant. Students work together, teams meet with other teams, students consult with the teacher, and experts are welcomed into the class, all in an effort to maximize positive interactions.

For the teacher, the workshop is a time for observation and documentation. Students will struggle with misconceptions and errors. Productive struggle can be beneficial, but frustration is discouraging. Ideally, teachers balance having students make their own way with targeted interventions as needed. Carefully monitoring the levels of engagement and student success will indicate the best times to conference with a learner or group of learners.

When planning for a workshop, teachers must consider the needs of all learners from all their potential starting points. Anticipating the pieces of the puzzle that students should know or be able to do in order to make sense of the new material allows teachers to build the scaffolds and supports into the adventure. It's of great importance to remember that learning is not linear. By creating a hypothetical learning trajectory, teachers can anticipate areas where students will get stuck and need support. Thus, the scaffolds, materials, mini-lessons, practice, and feedback can be pre-planned to some extent.

Through focused observations, workshops present the ideal conditions to uncover what students are thinking.

A workshop might involve:

- exploring a bike with tape measures, protractors, and timers.
- researching information about windmills and generating electricity to refine questions about the design of wind turbine blades.
- comparing bus routes and walking times in preparation for a trip to the museum.
- packing materials such as clipboards, tape measures, and protractors for a visit to the hardware store.
- preparing an information brochure and permission form for families.
- completing calculations.
- practising the manipulation of the formula for slope given different known values after a mini-lesson.

- sharing calculations and reasoning on chart papers with other teams.
- building toboggans out of cardboard.
- adding terms to the class vocabulary list.
- using floor tape to see the actual size of a proposed storage shed.
- comparing kitchen tools such as measuring cups and measuring spoons to discuss equivalent fractions and decimals.
- designing and building trundle wheels to fulfill a need for a long-distance measuring tool.
- reflecting on and organizing pictures for the Individual Learning Portfolios to self-assess our progress toward our goals.
- making clinometers for use in measuring the angle of elevation in the field.
- asking and answering questions about a solution presented by a classmate.
- researching guidelines for wheelchair ramps.
- practising the use of benchmarks to compare fractions.
- discussing proportions as a full class.
- preparing a written argument to defend a point of view.

Fieldwork

At the heart of expeditionary learning is fieldwork. It is during these expeditions into the community that students have the opportunity to consciously assume the role of mathematician. Where do mathematicians do their work? In the hardware store, at the zoo, in the grocery store, at the park, in a sports arena, at a construction site, and in all places where questions, wonderings, and problems live. While on-site, students become active investigators, using the research tools and techniques used by professionals in the field. Fieldwork is inspiring for learners as it places them directly inside a problem. They are no longer outsiders reading about a problem or spectators watching a lesson. They are the main characters in a learning adventure. Students interact with and respond to the elements of the situation.

Reacting in the field is consistent with Mason and Spence's (1999) view of knowing as knowing how to act in the moment when the information is immediately required. This knowing how to act is the culmination of knowing why, knowing how, knowing the technique, and knowing the process. This knowing is found within interactions between individuals and the elements; it is alive and evolving. As an essential component of expeditionary learning, fieldwork is intended to be risky and rewarding. Students and teachers find themselves in unfamiliar environments that "push people out of their comfort zones and force them to see themselves differently and start thinking differently about what they are capable of doing" (Lang, 2012, p. 75). This risk provides the uncertainty that cannot be matched in the classroom. Just as professionals dealing with unknowns develop an intuitive sense, fieldwork develops intuition in young learners so that they know how to respond when faced with a problematic situation. The lived experience in the field lets students construct for themselves a more complete understanding of the world around them.

Examples of fieldwork might include:

- launching student-made rockets to test how the angle of elevation at the launch affects the distance travelled.
- launching student-made rockets to test how the area of the wings affects flight time.
- interviewing the planetarium guides to learn about representing large numbers such as those numbers used to communicate distances in space and scientific notation.
- gathering measurements at a skateboard park (see above) to test how the steepness of a slope affects the speed of the skateboard and building a scale model of favourite features such as "the bowl" or "the wave."
- visiting the hardware store with the building plans for a storage shed to determine the amount of materials and cost.
- playing a round of mini-golf to determine how an understanding of angles can make you a better golfer.
- measuring enclosures at the zoo to compare these habitats with the natural range of animals to support an argument for or against zoos.
- measuring drum sets at the music store to find out how the volume of a drum affects the sound it produces.
- building scale models based on statues at an art gallery to investigate fractions, ratios and proportions.

- comparing prices and amounts at the grocery store to determine the best buys.
- measuring the speed (rate) of the skaters and the speed of slap shots at the hockey rink.
- investigating changes in populations and population density in the forest.
- measuring rate of growth at the community garden.
- using similar triangles to measure height at the football field.
- counting cars to determine the rate of CO_2 emissions.
- touring the neighbourhood looking for ramps and measuring rise and run to determine how steepness affects safety.
- studying populations of animals and plants in a local forested area to prepare arguments for and against a new housing development.

Developing intuition to navigate uncertainty requires educators to create authentic learning opportunities beyond their classrooms. Fieldwork offers students the chance to take on the role of the engineer in the kinds of environments where engineers do their learning and work. While onsite, students are active investigators, applying the research tools, techniques of inquiry, and standards of presentation used by professionals in the field. Being in the field pushes both the teacher and the learner to try new things that they may not have had the opportunity to try elsewhere. Roberts (2012) insists that "children must actively sense and feel their immediate surroundings and it is the educator's job to provide the freedom necessary for the child to follow his or her natural inclinations" (p. 33).

Measuring slope.

As mentioned earlier, fieldwork is intended to be risky and rewarding. A key element "of being a mathematical inquirer is traveling paths that are not well marked" (Whitin & Cox, 2003, p. 37). Through experiences out in the communities that surround their schools, students and teachers build stories to share that tell of their belonging. This on-location learning lets them know that what is sketched on the board or seen in a book can be experienced instead as a part of a living system. An expeditionary math classroom has no walls, no boundaries, and no limits: all spaces are learning places.

Mini-lessons and Conferences

Mathematicians are efficient. Algorithms, formal processes, and structures, once fully developed by the individual and deeply understood, can allow for more efficient work.

As teachers observe students, they note which aspects of the content each student is able to successfully master and which pieces are a challenge. Through questioning or in conversation with their teacher or peers, students may gain clarification; while, at other times, the correction may need to be more direct. A mini-lesson involves a small group of students for whom similar learning goals are a challenge. The lesson is targeted and short. It may include direct instruction from the teacher, the use of manipulatives or models, or it may be a demonstration problem that the teacher and students solve together. A mini-lesson is followed by practice. Practice can take the form of continued work with the manipulatives, a similar set of problems to solve (e.g., where the context stays the same, but the variables are given as different amounts), or as individual practice. This practice reviews the methods used to teach the concept, offers guided practice with supports, and then challenges the learner with independent questions. The type and amount of practice is variable and is decided with the student.

A mini-lesson is taught to individual students, student teams, or to the whole class as needed. Topics for these targeted small group or individual lessons are carefully selected to support learners "where they are at" in their thinking, allowing for the most variation in intent.

During a mini-lesson or conference, the teacher first explores what the students have uncovered. By asking guiding questions or by presenting new information, the teacher supports students in clarifying, making connections, and moving forward efficiently. This gives the teachers and the students an opportunity to transform invented strategies into more formal processes and efficient algorithms.

Topics for mini-lessons and conferences are purposefully selected based on ongoing formative assessment data. Intervening at appropriate times (once the students have had ample time to wrestle with a concept) is key. Intervening too soon may limit learning from productive failure; intervening too late may result in misconceptions that are tricky to resolve. A well-timed mini-lesson or conference gives students not only immediate, purposeful feedback, but also modelling, guided practice, and individual practice, resulting in a co-created, individualized learning path.

Moving between students and student groups creates a space for immediate assessment and feedback. Short conferences between students and teachers are used to clarify the learner's thinking for the learner, clarify the learner's thinking for the teacher, reveal where a misconception or misunderstanding is rooted, reveal where solid understandings have been made, draw out the learner's reasoning to better understand their process, highlight connections for the learner to prior knowledge, and determine the next steps for learning together. Conferencing with small groups and individual students in the moment, when the learning is happening, enables the teacher to personalize learning through differentiated materials, topics, and supports.

Conferencing about units of measure.

A mini-lesson or conference might involve:

- using tape measures to learn to convert between units of measure.
- learning to divide three-digit numbers using base-ten blocks.
- learning to compare fractions using a set of pattern blocks.
- learning to subtract using an open number line.
- learning to develop a formula such as the one needed to describe the relationship between the side lengths of a right triangle.
- learning to plot x and y coordinates to describe a slope.

Learning to Learn by Living the Math

When we live the math, we focus on being mathematicians and developing the habits of problem solvers, critical thinkers, innovators, and learners. Engagement with fieldwork, mini-lessons and conferences, and workshops offer students the opportunity to build their own processes. Commonalities exist among the processes employed by learners. When a curious or problematic situation is uncovered, learners explore, research, develop plans and ideas, create solutions, reason, communicate their solutions and their learning, make connections, and reflect upon their process. These are the strategies that we emphasize during expeditionary learning as these are the strategies that learners use. These strategies, although presented here in order, are not intended to be used in sequence. At times, students will find themselves using just one, while at other times they may feel they are using many at once. With practice, students will become familiar with the strengths of each strategy and naturally move between them, developing their own intuitive sense for learning. Their sequencing of the strategies is dependent upon their varied purposes.

Explore

Mathematicians wonder. They observe their surroundings: the interactions, the changes, and the processes that are taking place. Their observations form the basis of their questions. The complex nature of interactions necessitates that mathematicians examine problems from multiple perspectives. They hypothesize, making reasonable predictions based on initial evidence and past experiences, as a way to guide their thinking. In expeditionary learning, exploring signals the start of a new adventure. As students explore, they wonder about the dynamics of a situation. They observe. They estimate, using known referents, facts, benchmarks, and by building onto insights from past experiences. They identify curious situations and pose questions. These initial questions deconstruct the situation, pulling pieces apart so that all factors, parameters, limitations, boundaries, and possibilities are exposed. Students gather initial data, noting what is known to them now and what they will need to learn. This exploration leads to an understanding of the need for a solution and allows for the creation of solution criteria. Students are asked to make connections to past experiences and problems that are similar as well as to those that are not similar. This exploring phase is emphasized by Zull (2001), who notes that "all members of the community can serve as teachers and all buildings as schools" (p. 44), and by Martinez and Stager (2013), who add that "students engaged in direct experience with materials, unforeseen obstacles, and serendipitous discoveries may result in understanding never anticipated by the teacher" (p. 52).

Example: Outdoor Drums
While exploring an outdoor playground, students became interested in a set of drums (see right). They compared the sounds, informally measured the height, diameter, and circumference with their hands, shared ideas, and tried to play a song together. They wondered:

- "Which drum is the biggest?"
- "How come the sounds change from drum to drum?"
- "Is there a pattern? Do they always get taller by the same amount?"
- "Do real drum sets work this way too?"
- "Can we build a drum set like this at school?"

Each of these questions is exactly the kind of question we hoped for. The more open and indistinct the problem, the greater potential for innovation, creativity, and meaningful, personalized learning. To explore these questions further, students will have to formalize a definition of "biggest" in terms of heights, circumference, or volume. They will need to create a plan for comparing the sound and size of the drums and describe the pattern using measurement. They will need to find a drum set either at the school or at a local music store to investigate, and form a plan that includes the size, scale, materials, cost, and timeline for constructing their own drum set.

Example: Accessible Dance

When asked to design a wheelchair ramp that would make our school's second floor dance studio accessible for all, students needed to explore:

- the *height* of the dance studio.
- the *slope* and design of other ramps in the neighbourhood.
- the safety guidelines for *steepness* of slope used for wheelchairs.
- the *angle of elevation* that would result in the safest slope.
- how to physically measure the angle of elevation with a *clinometer*.
- how to calculate the *angle* when two other variables are measured.
- the *distance* the ramp would extend from the base of the building, and whether this was an acceptable distance or if the ramp needed to include turns.
- the *area of the arc* needed to turn the wheelchair.
- how to draw a *scale* diagram to communicate their design.
- the *cost* of materials and managing a *budget*.

It is important to note that developing a problem statement, such as "What is the relationship between the size of the drum and the sound it produces?", is an essential part of the learning process. Students will need time to build this skill. If the problem statement is not well-defined, carry on. As students work through their problem, there will be opportunities to revisit the initial statement, making adjustments and improvements. Students will keep track of the changes so that they can reflect on these decisions as part of their learning stories and refine their questioning techniques.

Research

Research in expeditionary learning consists of identifying the measurements, data, observations, and information needed to work toward a solution. Students may need to research information about the context, the physical geography of the space, the scientific processes present, the mathematical content, contributing factors, or possible similar solutions. Information is gathered from a variety of sources including reference materials, technology, experts in the field, and other classmates. Students enter into the problem to gather information through measuring, observing, and analyzing. They evaluate the information and make decisions about its relevance to the solution and the reliability of the source. By creating a purpose for research, students themselves learn to define the variables.

To be successful at this stage, students must maintain a balance of both innovative personal strategies and known strategies with formal processes and algorithms. The learners also identify information that might be helpful in their process, but that is not yet known to them. For example, students may realize that the desired solution requires that they find the area of a triangle. They've already worked with the concept of area and are able to apply the formula for finding the area of a rectangle. The next step is to develop a strategy for determining the area of the triangle by counting, knowing that a formula must exist and that the formula will provide them with the most efficient path to the solution. The students then set out to develop and verify a formula to calculate the area of a triangle.

For example, a standard written problem might ask students to find the unit price for one can of soup when six cans of soup are sold together for $8.25. Here the students are given the two variables: price and amount. They need to divide the total cost by the number of cans and record their answer.

As participants in an expeditionary problem, however, students would have to decide what they want to buy, and what information they need to be able to determine the unit price or the better buy. They have to first decide that they want to buy the soup and how much soup they want. They then have to find the cost of the soup, compare the price for the six cans with the price for one can, identify a strategy for their calculations, and determine which is the better buy. They have to be able to justify that the information they gathered is accurate and has been collected in the best way – thinking about what tools they need, how to use those tools, and whether or not their numbers make sense. They might find that they've gathered information from a number of sources including reference materials, technology, experts in the field, and other classmates. This soup example may include customer loyalty rewards or discounts, storage space, a brand preference, and the purpose of the soup. Here, the topic and concepts to be learned are "on demand" and relevant to the students' own questions rather than according to the next chapter in the text.

Develop

This planning stage invites learners to suggest multiple strategies and processes without judgment. Innovative and creative strategies uniquely designed for the specific problem are welcomed, as are strategies and processes that have been successfully used in the past for questions that have similar features. Each proposed strategy and process is evaluated in terms of its potential success. A plan for deepening understanding and acquiring new knowledge is also made. This plan includes a detailed list of the data to be collected, such as measurements of length, time, and amount, as well as the formulas to try and the steps to follow. The plan includes a list of tools, such as measuring tapes, clipboards, paper, and a pencil, as well as a short description of how information will be gathered. Collaborative student teams plan for the active involvement of all members by sharing their own strengths and goals. Teams also sketch a timeline, identifying benchmarks to complete and likely due dates. The final plan is checked against the initial solution criteria to make sure it will take them in the direction of the solution.

Choices in the planning stage are intended to empower students. Setting the direction for their learning cultivates confidence and persistence. Plans remain in development throughout the process, and are constantly re-evaluated and adjusted. Adjustments are not considered mistakes or errors. Instead, they are seen as incredibly useful in zeroing in on the best possible solution. Getting stuck, being puzzled, and doubling back are all useful trials that will, at some point, offer greater clarity and confidence. Developing the plan is a complex stage with multiple viewpoints coming together and an extensive list of possibilities to consider.

The plan also includes a description of how each member of the team will contribute to the learning of the group as well as work toward personal learning goals. Strong communication skills and a positive team environment allow the team to arrive at a mutual understanding of what each member has in mind. The positives and negatives of each plan are discussed until the team reaches some accord. A team may settle on one plan or agree to try several approaches and compare the results.

Consider the following example. A set of stands had recently been built at our local football field. As a class, we walked over to the field to explore this new addition. While there, the students wondered how many fans could sit in the

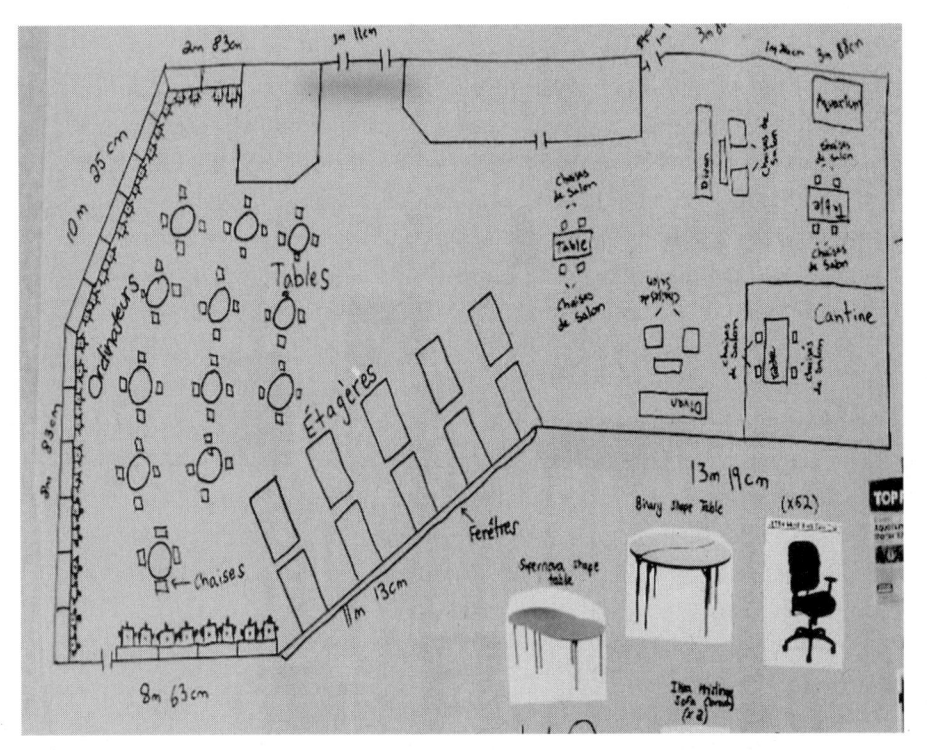

Student-created plan for library.

stands. In teams, students turned their initial wondering into preliminary plans. The first team organized themselves as follows:

- **Student 1** directed the gathering of information and recorded it for the team.
- **Student 2** counted the total number of benches and shared the information with Student 1, so that it was recorded.
- **Student 3** measured the length of five benches to verify that they were the same length and shared the measurements with Student 1 to be recorded.
- **Student 2** then sat on the bench so that **Student 3** could measure the length of bench needed for one person to sit.
- **Student 3** then sat on the bench so that **Student 2** could measure the length of the bench occupied by **Student 3**.

Another team chose to implement a different plan, as follows:

- **Student 1** directed the gathering and recording of the information.
- **Students 2** and **3** sat side by side starting at the edge of one bench.
- **Student 2** then moved to the other side of **Student 3,** who then moved to the other side of **Student 2**, and so on.

This way, they counted the number of people who could comfortably fit on a bench. The process was then repeated on four other benches to make sure that the benches would hold the same number of people. The total number of benches was then counted so that the number of fans per bench could be multiplied by the total number of benches.

The ideal plan is structured enough to provide a starting point and flexible enough to be adjusted in the moment to maximize learning.

Create and Construct

At this stage, learners are encouraged to experiment with new strategies and processes. The plan is adjusted as needed and includes creative and innovative ideas that arise spontaneously during the process. Consequently, careful attention is given to the development of persistence during this stage. While errors can be frustrating, time-consuming, and overwhelming, it is important to create a habit of dealing with errors as opportunities. The realization that a path or strategy pursued is not a correct one further supports the students' justification for selecting a more efficient and more effective path. A mistake is an invitation to examine what is wrong, retrace steps until the last truth is

Constructing models.

found, and move forward again with more confidence. To welcome and anticipate errors, teachers continuously monitor the level of engagement and satisfaction in the students and adjust the length and depth of the problem as needed. Discoveries and innovations made by wiggling the plan are celebrated because learning is "not about arriving somewhere expected, but about deliberately moving outside of what is known" (Zull, 2011, p. 67).

The create-and-construct stage is ideal for individual, small-group, and full-class mini-lessons and conferences. While the teacher observes students working through calculations, misunderstandings and misconceptions come to light. It's at this time that students make visible their understanding of, and ability with, mathematical concepts. Selecting the right moment to intervene, while still giving enough time for productive struggle, means that the teacher needs to know the learners well. The teacher provides a high level of support to students as they learn to persist, sticking with a problem until they reach a solution.

Example: At the Movies
When students got interested in knowing how much popcorn was popped in a day at a Silver City Cinemas location, students organized a trip to the theatre. While there, they measured the popcorn machine, timed the popping cycle, and collected small, medium, and large popcorn bags.

Back at the school, they built a full-size model popcorn machine out of cardboard. Using photos they'd taken at the movie theatre, they reasoned that one cycle filled one third of the machine. They measured one third of the height of the model and calculated the volume. Knowing that there were five machines at the theatre, they multiplied this volume by five. To find the total volume popped each day, they found that it took four minutes for each pop cycle, or 15 cycles per hour (60 minutes divided by 4 = 15). Multiplying the hours the theatre is open each day (10 AM until 12 PM = 14 hours) by 15 pop cycles by the volume of the five machines gave the total volume popped each day. The students realized that popped popcorn would not completely fill the space in the popping machine and there are some times when the machine is not running, so they wanted to test another process.

At the theatre, students learned that the concession uses a scoop of kernels for each popcorn batch. They counted the number of tablespoons of kernels needed to fill one scoop. Then they counted the number of kernels in one tablespoon. To find the total number of kernels popped, they multiplied the number of kernels in one tablespoon by the number of tablespoons in one scoop by the number of cycles of popcorn. They wanted to know what this amount of popcorn looked like, so they filled the large, medium, and small bags with popcorn and counted the number of cups needed to fill each one. Then they counted the number of pieces in one cup. They found the total number of pieces in each bag by multiplying the number of pieces in one cup by the number of cups in one bag.

Measuring volume of popcorn bag.

The students wondered how much money the theatre made from selling popcorn. They wrote possible equations for the number of bags of popcorn of each size that the theatre could sell in a day. Once the equations balanced the volume of popcorn popped with the volume of the bags, they used the prices to find how much they would have to pay to buy all that popcorn. Students then researched the markup on movie theatre popcorn and used this percentage to find the total amount that the theatre earned by selling popcorn.

Throughout the experience, students had to find their own starting points and identify new learning that was needed. When new understandings were taking shape, students would conference with the teacher. This could look like a mini-lesson, where the teacher and students have a specific learning goal in mind and the teacher supports students with questions, examples, and practice. For example, some students might find measuring the cinema popcorn machine a challenge. The teacher would work with that group to review units of measure and how to gather accurate measurements. This mini-lesson could be followed by some specific practice whereby students reinforce the new skill.

Some students might not be familiar with the formula to calculate volume and so would conference with the teacher to explore the concept and develop the formula using manipulatives. Students would then have the opportunity to practice, using models. Once students become confident with the concept, they can hop back into the problem and apply their new skills.

This technique creates a fluid model for learning. Students are immersed in the problem to solve, but are supported with mini-lessons and conferences as needed. They flow in and out of their problem situation, and balance building their solution with mini-lessons and conferences.

Connect

Understanding can be imagined as a complex web of ties between ideas. Highlighting these connections with learners allows them to see that what they study in school does not come neatly packaged into subject area binders. A key element in understanding content is the ability to connect it to experiences. Strong learners demonstrate multidisciplinary thinking, the ability to incorporate ideas from the humanities, mathematics, language, and science, and the ability to transfer knowledge from one situation to another. Making connections and transferring knowledge involves adopting new perspectives and seeing situations through new eyes.

Connecting Through One Context

While at The Forks, a historic meeting place at the junction of Winnipeg's two rivers, students noticed that the exterior of the Children's Museum is decorated with square tiles.

Wanting to know how many tiles were needed, students counted the number of rows and columns. They recalled that they'd already used arrays in class as a multiplication strategy, making it unnecessary to count each individual square. They made a quick sketch and measured one of the tiles.

In class, students used tiles to model the sides of the museum and drew arrays. They then developed a formula using the number of tiles in each row, calling this length, and the number of tiles in each column, calling this height.

Returning to a photo taken at The Forks, they wondered if they could apply this new formula to find the surface area of the Human Rights Museum, which uses rectangular tiles instead of square ones.

Human rights musuem (above); classroom-created array (below).

Reason

Reasoning involves synthesizing new and old ideas, refining thinking, deciding what is important and what is not, and putting all the ideas together in a way that makes sense to the learner and can be shared with others as proof of new discovery. The ability to reason, to develop a "line of thought adopted to produce assertions and reach conclusions" (Boesen, Lithner, & Palm, 2010, p. 92), develops through appropriate experiences. Experiences that include positive arguments and productive conflict are energizing. As students learn to reason, they examine patterns in solutions. They construct relationships between representations and the lived problem scenario. Students accept or reject the solution. As mathematicians, students "reflect on the context in which the problem arose, to decide if something unexpected has arisen, to raise further questions, or in some other way to enrich or extend knowledge" (Watson, 2008, p. 3). They construct an argument based on past experiences and new learning. They search for counterexamples.

In addition, a fundamental aspect of thinking like a learner occurs when students engage in the practice of explaining to themselves and others why a discovery is true or how widely a new theory can be applied. In order for a teacher to understand a student's thinking when assessing their reasoning, the teacher needs assessment tasks that reveal not only the student's factual knowledge, but also how they connect that information to other ideas, and when and how they use it (Schoenfeld, 1992). Schoenfeld goes on to explain that when assessing a student's decision making and reasoning, the teacher needs to know what options the student had available. That is, did a student fail to pursue particular options because they overlooked them, or was the student completely unaware those paths existed?

Example: At the Movies
While investigating the number of seats available and the cost of tickets at the movie theatre, students wondered why each seat shared an armrest with its neighbour. What would need to happen for there to be two armrests per chair? To find out, students measured the width and length of the theatre. They counted the number of seats in each row and the number of rows. They then designed and built a cardboard and duct-tape prototype of a new, two-armrest theatre chair. The new chair included one armrest with a built-in drink holder and the other armrest with a built-in popcorn bag holder. Using the new chair dimensions, they calculated the number of two-armrest chairs that would fill a theatre row. Students wrote letters to the theatre manager pitching their two-armrest chairs idea, reasoning that, although the total number of seats available

would decrease, the cost of the tickets could be increased, since patrons would most certainly be willing to pay far more for a more comfortable seat. They included detailed measurements of the theatre and the original chairs, and a scale diagram of the movie theatre with the number of rows and the number of chairs in each row clearly shown. They also included another scale diagram, with ratio calculations of the improved two-armrest chair. Their written report consisted of an explanation of why they found the original theatre chairs inadequate and their suggestion for improvements. It gave their rationale for the two armrests and the popcorn holder. Their response contained calculations, words, images, and models, and shared the story of their learning. Such a response is much more than simply an answer.

Communicate

Each of us comes with our own lens through which we view the world. Our interpretation of events is shaped by our past. Communicating an experience to others is vital in building a common understanding and a shared solution. Learning is a process of social construction and requires that, as learners, we share what we've learned so that we can all learn together.

A focus on communication skills serves a number of purposes. First, effective communication is required as students interact and collaborate with peers during the learning process. In the planning stage, students generate ideas for the active involvement of all members of their group. In doing so, they commit to sharing their strengths and drawing out the strengths of others. Each student is responsible for making meaningful contributions to discussions aimed at shared understandings. They learn to present new ideas and to respond to new ideas presented by their classmates. All students make an effort to understand each other's strategies and solutions. They learn to respectfully express opinions and consider the opinions of others. A learning community that values the diverse contributions of all its members fosters confidence.

Second, ideas, insights, and experiences are strongest when they are shared. Students need opportunities to communicate solutions to the group and to audiences beyond their classroom. The audience adds an extra challenge as students need to select appropriate language, symbols, models, and presentation formats that will convey their solution without sacrificing the integrity of the math. A mathematical solution includes justifications, reasoning, correct units, labelled diagrams, tables, charts, and other representational tools. Formal mathematical terminology and standard units help all audiences come to a common understanding.

Example: Are Zoos Ethical?

When the local media reported that the zoo would be hosting a penguin exhibit, students were outraged. They wondered how penguins could live in Winnipeg, as it would certainly be too hot. These questions quickly opened a debate as to whether or not penguins, or any animal, should be kept in a zoo. Looking to develop and then defend their opinion, the students and I planned a trip to the zoo. While there, students measured and examined enclosures, interviewed zookeepers, made models to analyze animal behavior, and investigated conservation activities. They prepared a presentation for the zookeepers in which they stated their opinion and shared supporting evidence, including a comparison between the zoo enclosure and the natural range of the animal, the impact of the reduced area, and the animal's speed, jumping ability, or wingspan, changes in life expectancy, and diet.

Example: Musical Mathematicians

When a local music store posted a billboard encouraging parents to enroll their children in music lessons and claiming that those who play the piano are better at math, we had to investigate. We decided we needed to speak with some musical experts and planned a trip to the local high school to interview the band. As a class, we created a list of questions about how math might be helpful to musicians and in making music. We recorded our questions on chart paper. We wondered:

- Can you hear the difference between a whole note, a half note, a quarter note, and an eighth note?
- How does the length of a note change when the time signature changes?
- Is it true that the longer the instrument is, the lower the sound?
- How do you know where the notes are on a guitar?
- How does the sound of the drum change as the drum gets bigger?

We gathered information about travel times to and from the high school and created a schedule for our trip. We prepared our materials: recording sheets, cameras, rulers, tape measures, and timers. Once at the high school, we listened to the band play a few songs. A team of students measured the positions of a

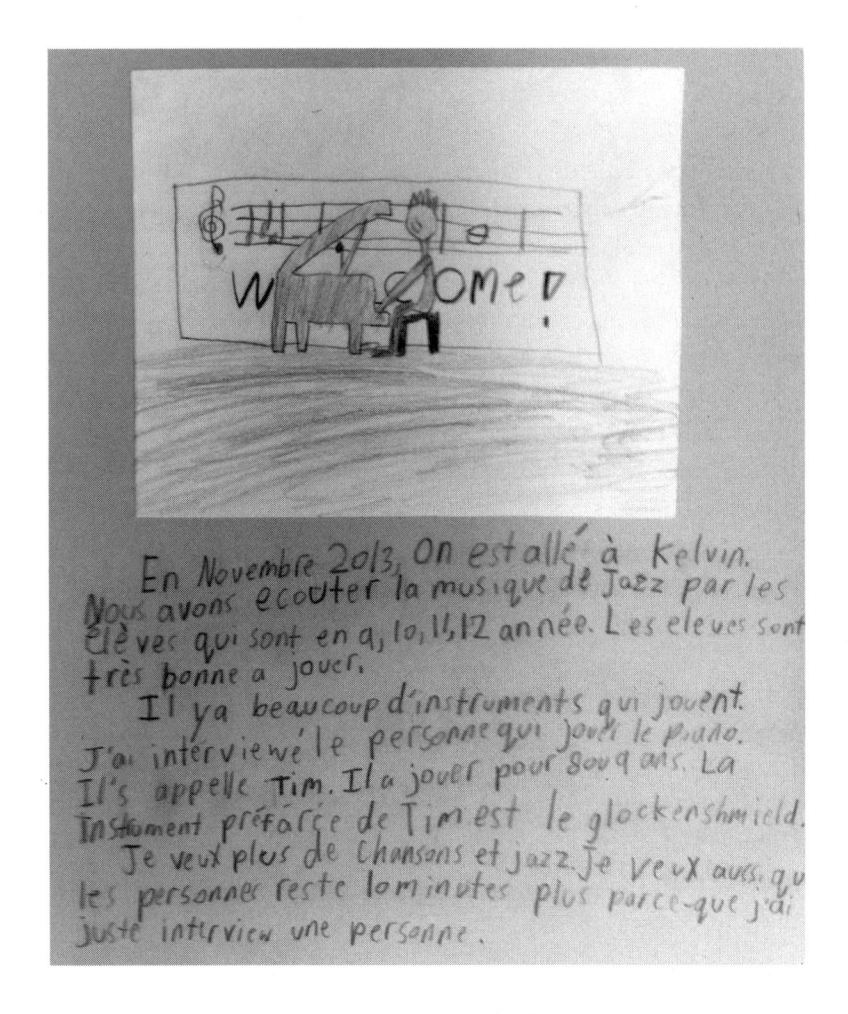

> En Novembre 2013, On est allé à kelvin.
> Nous avons ecouter la musique de Jazz par les
> élèves qui sont en 9, 10, 11, 12 année. Les eleves sont
> très bonne a jouer.
>   Il y a beaucoup d'instruments qui jouent.
> J'ai interviewé le personne qui joue le piano.
> Il's appelle Tim. Il a jouer pour 8ou9 ans. La
> Instrument préforcée de Tim est le glockenshmield.
>   Je veux plus de Chansons et jazz. Je veux auss, qu
> les personnes reste 10 minutes plus parce-que j'ai
> juste interview une personne.

trombone. They found that there are seven positions; the musician estimated the distance between positions to be two inches. We knew that inches are a unit of measure, but did not have any experience with them. We recorded the information and planned to research inches when we returned to class.

We explored the lengths of the xylophone keys and wondered how their lengths could be compared. We measured the keys and interviewed the musician. Once back in our classroom, we built paper models and discovered a pattern of fractional values.

We examined sheet music with a musician. We heard whole notes, half notes, quarter notes, and eighth notes. While reading the music, we identified different combinations of notes that produce a whole measure. We saw that two half notes make a whole, four quarter notes make a whole, and eight eighth notes make a whole. This led us to reason that two quarter notes make a half note and four eighth notes make a quarter note.

While examining the strings of a guitar, we wanted to know if they corresponded with the same fractional values we had assigned to the water-bottle notes. We measured the guitar and asked the musician some questions. More research was needed and so, once we returned to school, we continued to search for details. Students watched videos online and connected with staff members who played the guitar as well as our music teacher. We then constructed our own guitars, using our fractional values, some cardboard, elastics, and lots of staples. Students were able to play a familiar tune and could hear how the sound was different at different lengths of the elastics.

Many of us were immediately interested in the drum set. We wondered how the size of the drum affected the sound. After a spirited discussion we agreed that by size we meant volume. We then gathered the necessary measurements and sketched the drums. We asked the musicians to play each drum so that they could rate the sounds as high, medium, or low. Once back at the school, we researched how to calculate the volume of a cylinder.

Each team presented their solution on posters (such as the one, left) so that everyone could try each team's problem. Team members were the experts, answering questions and offering support while their classmate tried to find the same solution.

For the musicians, students wrote articles explaining how a knowledge of mathematics can help someone to be a great musician and help us to appreciate music as an art.

Reflect

Students and teachers are constantly encouraged to evaluate their learning, processes, and strategies. During an expedition or while in a workshop, mini-lesson, or conference setting, students are encouraged to make adjustments to their plans as new discoveries lead them to better understandings. Growth is evident when ineffective strategies are replaced with more efficient and accurate ones. Reasons for doing so should be explored. Through conversations, presentations, products, and actions, students can share what and how they have learned. Portfolios and learning stories are also used to promote self-reflection and goal setting. The purpose of reflection is to commit learners to ongoing growth, honour their achievements, and share their learning with their communities. A learning story is a retelling of how a learner has made sense of the world and their experience of problem solving (Egan, 1998). A learning story is a collection of photos and examples of student learning from inquiry question to successful solution. Snapshots of students while learning are extremely valuable when teaching students to reflect. Each picture serves as a visual reminder of the experience and the personal feelings they evoke. The stories are talking props that students can revisit when looking for ideas for solving a new problem and when asked to talk about their learning.

A learning story serves many purposes. First, it is a student's own retelling of events through which they have learned new techniques, skills, or content. The story belongs to the student and so represents their autonomy and ownership of their learning. The learning story is the student's own perspective on their learning: what helped them to learn, what didn't, what actions they took and why. Consequently, students and teachers are able to look back and revisit mistakes with the confidence of knowing that they now have a successful solution. In other words, they can identify missteps, misunderstandings, and misconceptions, and discuss why they were unsuccessful. Perhaps most importantly, these reflections are a visual reminder of commitment to their learning community. No one has gone about their learning alone. All learners have contributed to the shared knowledge of the group, just as all have enjoyed personal successes. Fieldwork, mini-lessons, and workshops create an interwoven fabric of mathematical knowledge, skill, competencies, and strategies. It is difficult to separate these experiences into strands and individual outcomes. These pictures and captions are very telling as to the comfort level learners have developed around content. Regular review of the portfolios offers key insights for planning and targeted mini-lessons.

No two stories will be the same. Because the initial question was open-ended, and its answers unknown, each story branches out toward meaningful learning for each student. The story is a tool for assessing learning for both educators and learners. Mistakes are included as loops and detours when learners pursue a path that didn't take them where they'd originally planned. Scaffolds such as organization frames, planning templates, and checklists are included in the story. The strategies and processes of the learner, such as using an area model to compare fractions, finding a common denominator, or converting to a decimal value, are to be retold with as much detail as possible. These strategies and processes serve as evidence of reasoning and thinking that will support the teacher in assessment and support learners next time they find themselves challenged by a new problem. The depth to which each story conveys that the learner has found meaning and purpose in the experience will let both teacher and learner judge the inclusive nature of the expedition.

In one learning story, a student retold his journey from question to new learning. He noted that, when asked to create a plan for a universally accessible entrance to a second-floor dance studio, he was puzzled. He and his teammates weren't sure where to start. They explored the staircase, took some initial measurements, and created a few possible sketches of straight ramps. They researched the government safety standards for the angle of incline for a wheelchair ramp and built a small-scale model. They then returned to the staircase and measured the distance that the ramp would extend, and realized that it would extend well into the street in front of the school. As a result, the student noted that they changed plans and made a design that incorporated turns. Because they were not sure how much space a wheelchair needed to make a turn, they tested out a chair. They had to calculate the area needed for the platforms. All along, the student had included calculations of slope, ratio, and measurement conversions. In conversation with the student, the process of problem solving was revealed. He and his partner first explored the situation, then wondered, researched, planned, and wondered some more. They calculated the created model, then made connections to what they already knew about scale, ratio, triangles, and angles into new learning about slope. The learning story is evidence of reflection and serves as a conversation starter for a more in-depth discussion of how a student has gone about their learning.

What I Have Learned by Living the Math

- We create unity through learning in a community to which all students feel that they belong.
- Shared experiences create stories to tell, memories to hold on to, and knowledge to build on.
- Fieldwork brings content to life with sounds, smell, touch, and emotion – we live the math.

- We tailor these learning experiences so that each student is working on appropriate content with available scaffolding and embedded extensions.
- Knowledge is not a commodity to be collected; it is an event.
- Confidence and persistence are cultivated by having students define their own goals and their own learning paths.
- Learning is strongest when fieldwork, workshops, and mini-lessons are interconnected, linking personal experience, theory, and practice to maximize the connectedness.
- No single learning strategy is effective for all learners all the time. The built-in variety of fieldwork, mini-lesson, and workshop opens a range of learning options.
- Teaming with classmates who bring different areas of expertise to the group develops in each learner an appreciation of their own strengths and of the strengths of others.
- Mathematics is best learned when the interconnectedness of topics and skills is highlighted.
- Knowing how to act in the moment is a combination of knowing what and knowing why.
- The timing of a mini-lesson is critical and should occur spontaneously when the student reaches a point where the outcome of the lesson steps them into their zone of proximal development (Vygotsky, 1978).
- Learning has no boundaries.
- Every space is a learning place. Everyone is a learner.

References

Boesen, J., Lithner, J., & Palm, T. (2010). The relation between types of assessment tasks and the mathematical reasoning students use. *Educational Studies in Mathematics, 75*(1), 89-105. Retrieved from http://dx.doi.org/10.1007./s10649-010-9242-9

Boss, S. (2012). *Bringing innovation to school: Empowering students to thrive in a changing world.* Bloomington, IN: Solution Tree Press.

Brooks, J., & Brooks, M. (1999). *In search of understanding: The case for constructivist classrooms.* Alexandria, VA: Association for Supervision and Curriculum Development.

Dufour, R., & Dufour, R. (2010). The role of professional learning communities in advancing 21st century skills. In J. Bellanca & R. Brandt (Eds.), *21st century skills.* Bloomington, IN: Solution Tree Press.

Egan, G. (1998). *The skilled helper: A problem management approach to helping.* Pacific Grove, CA: Brooks/Cole Publishing Company.

Gardner, H. (2008). *Five minds for the future.* Boston, MA: Harvard Business Press.

Hayes Jacobs, H. (2010). *Curriculum 21: Essential education for a changing world.* Alexandria, VA: ASCD.

Katz, J. (2013). *Resource teachers: A changing role in the three-block model of universal design for learning.* Winnipeg, MB: Portage & Main Press.

Lang, A. (2012). *The power of why.* Toronto, ON: HarperCollins Publishers Ltd.

MacLeod, G. (2016). *Expeditionary learning for inclusive education.* Winnipeg, MB: University of Manitoba.

Martinez, S., & Stager, G. (2013). *Invent to learn: Making, tinkering, and engineering in the classroom.* Torrance, CA: Constructing Modern Knowledge Press.

Mason, J., and Spence, M. (1999). Beyond mere knowledge of mathematics: The importance of knowing to act in the moment. Educational Studies in Mathematics, 38, 135-161.

Roberts, J. (2012). *Beyond learning by doing: Theoretical currents in experiential education.* New York, NY: Routledge.

Schoenfeld, A. H. (1992). Learning to think mathematically: Problem solving, metacognition, and sense-making in mathematics. In D. Grouws (Ed.), *Handbook for research on mathematics teaching and learning* (pp. 334-370). New York, NY: MacMillan.

Vygotsky, L. (1978). *Mind in society: The development of higher psychological processes* (14th ed.). Cambridge, MA: Harvard University Press.

Wagner, T., & Dintersmith, T. (2015). *Most likely to succeed: Preparing our kids for the innovation era.* New York, NY: Simon and Schuster.

Watson, A. (2008). School mathematics as a special kind of mathematics. *For the Learning of Mathematics, 28,* 3-7. Retrieved from https://flm-journal.org/Articles/flm_28-3_Watson.pdf

Whitin, D., & Cox, R. (2003). *A mathematical passage: Strategies for promoting inquiry.* Portsmouth, NH: Heinemann.

Zull J. (2011). *From brain to mind: Using neuroscience to guide change in education.* Sterling, VA: Stylus Publishing.

About the Author
Laura Sims, PhD, is an associate professor in the Faculty of Education, Université de Saint-Boniface, Winnipeg. She teaches courses related to cultural diversity in education as well as integrating Indigenous perspectives into education. In her research, she specializes in education for sustainability and community-based assessment processes. Laura taught high school for 10 years in Winnipeg and in the Dominican Republic. For three years, she managed a Canadian International Development Agency environmental project in Central America.

Who Should Read This Chapter?
Educators, formal and nonformal, who are interested in learning about how educational concepts like project-based learning are used in international development contexts to help people transition to more sustainable livelihoods.

The Theme of This Chapter in Three Words
Learning, international development.

As an Educator, What Are You Passionate About?
I am passionate about using education to facilitate a transition through which we learn to live more sustainably, respectfully, justly, and gently on this earth and with others (human and other-than-human beings).

CHAPTER 5

Insights from a Central American Agro-Conservation International Development Project

Laura Sims, Université de Saint-Boniface
St. Boniface, Winnipeg, Manitoba, Canada

Introduction

According to Larmer, Mergendoller, and Boss (2015), project-based learning involves asking critical questions, and providing opportunities for sustained inquiry, creative thinking, and problem solving around complex real-life challenges that are relevant to learners' lives. The learning process is to be collaborative, with learners having a voice in decision making around certain aspects of process and content. The underlying intent is that learners can apply skills and information acquired through a project-based learning process to situations they face in their lives, including their professional lives.

Between 2006 and 2013, I was involved as project manager and later as collaborator and researcher with a Central American community-based pest-management project funded by the Canadian International Development Agency (CIDA). The goal of the project was to promote safer, and alternative-to-chemical, pest-management strategies to small-scale farmers in Honduras, Costa Rica, and Nicaragua. The aim was to enable a transition toward more sustainable agricultural practices. The project involved collaborators from three Central American universities, students, small-scale farmers, and other stakeholders.

Project implementation was planned collaboratively with the Central American teams; subsequently, the project activities were implemented by these national teams according to local needs in collaboration with participating farmers. Throughout the planning and implementation process, there was ongoing critical reflection on challenges and next steps; national teams supported one another in the process, addressing a regional issue through local interventions. Project activities included, but were not limited to, student practicums in rural communities, outreach workshops, farm demonstration and experimental plots, and a final symposium.

In this chapter, I explore how this Central American community-based agro-conservation project represents the essence of project-based learning. The project involved communities coming together locally and regionally around serious health and environmental issues: indiscriminate pesticide usage and inadequate handling and storage practices that resulted in negative health and environmental impacts. Project participants, who were local farmers and community members, became educators for one another in their spheres of influence and within their knowledge domains. They supported the inquiry process: solving problems and experimenting together, and planning activities according to participants' needs, interests, and local contexts. Describing the essential components of this CIDA project, and exploring and reflecting upon them through a project-based learning pedagogical lens, will help shed light on the commonalities and distinctions between how this approach might be applied in a classroom setting and how a similar approach has been used in a development context to promote education for sustainability with adult learners.

Specifically, in Part 1, I begin by introducing, in broad terms, the concepts of project-based learning and providing an overview of the CIDA project. In Parts 2 and 3, I provide a detailed description of the CIDA project, including how it was designed and implemented. In Part 4, I consider the essential project-based learning design elements followed by an exploration of how these elements occurred through the CIDA project. Part 5 focuses on the similarities and distinctions between project-based learning as it occurs in a classroom context as compared to an international development context.

Description of CIDA Pest Management Project[1]

As described in Sims (2016), through CIDA's "Community-based pest management in Central American agriculture" project, which lasted from 2006 to 2013, universities collaborated with rural communities and other stakeholders to increase food security through better pest-management practices. This project resulted from the observations of Dr. Annemieke Farenhorst, a professor in the Department of Soil Science at the University of Manitoba, who was on a research trip to Costa Rica and noticed farmers applying pesticides and employing unsafe practices (e.g., using no protective gear, spraying into the wind). Later she came to realize that these practices were a problem throughout the region. Dr. Farenhorst subsequently developed a proposal to address the issue, along with Costa Rican, Nicaraguan, and Honduran counterparts. The four participating universities were the Universidad de Costa Rica, Universidad Nacional Autónoma de Honduras, Universidad Nacional Agraria (Nicaragua), and the University of Manitoba (Canada). Each university put together a national team of diverse professionals from their institution that took on responsibilities within each of the project components. Funding was provided by CIDA under its University Partnerships in Cooperation and Development Program. As detailed in the project's final narrative report (Mulock & Herrera, 2013), more than 2200 participants from academia, government, rural communities, and local organizations were involved.

The project involved three main components. Each component included at least one representative from each national team and a wide breadth of professional fields of expertise. The *community development component* worked in rural communities with farm families to understand how and why they farm the way they do, with particular focus on their pest management practices. The *technical component* implemented farm demonstration plots and facilitated educational outreach activities. The aim of these activities was to provide alternatives to pesticide use and to promote safer pesticide storage, handling, and use. CIDA project activities also built on technical capacities through furnishing lab equipment to the three Central America universities and by

---

1   This description of the CIDA project, including the description of how project activities were designed and implemented, closely reflects information published in Sims (2016) that explores the learning outcomes resulting from participation in the project.

providing specific academic course work to the university collaborators. The *policy component* included the development of indicators to help understand current practices and monitor change over time. (For more project details see www.umanitoba.ca/afs/centralamerica_cbpm.) By way of meaningful participatory processes[2], CIDA project successes included increased engagement in decision making and environmental governance (Chibi, 2011).

Designing and Implementing CIDA Pest-Management Project Activities

As with project-based learning in the classroom, learners should be involved in the decision-making process about certain aspects of the learning process. So too in international development and natural resource and environmental management (NREM) projects if they are to be truly participatory and responsive to local needs and concerns (Diduck, Sinclair, Hostetler, & Fitzpatrick, 2012; Sims, 2012). Indeed, as argued in Sims (2016, p. 4), "the importance of the design of public involvement in NREM processes with respect to learning outcomes, sustainability, empowerment, and creating culturally-sensitive equitable decision-making forums cannot be overstated" (Muro and Jeffery 2008; Rist et al. 2007).

As the Canadian community-development team member (2007–2013) and CIDA project manager (2007–2010), I was in a privileged position, as I was able to guide project-planning activities between university collaborators. It was my responsibility to facilitate the inter-national workshops.[3] My involvement coincided with the beginning of the planning and implementation of the community-based activities. In order to enable a learning-focused, equitable, and potentially empowering process, I built upon prior research by intentionally integrating the ideal conditions for learning and a participatory approach (see Sims, 2012; Sinclair, Sims, & Spaling, 2009) into the design and facilitation of the CIDA inter-national planning workshops. Attempting to create the "ideal conditions for learning" in a planning process was meant to help mitigate potential power imbalances. These

---

2 These participatory processes (e.g., inter-national planning meetings) are described in detail in the following section.
3 "Inter-national" refers to activities that involved the different national teams.

kinds of opportunities to build upon and apply best practices in NREM planning processes, particularly ones integrating learning theory, are rare and considered innovative (Spaling, Montes, & Sinclair, 2011).

Drawing on my experiences as an educator of over twenty years and on relevant research, I intended the inter-national workshops to be designed from a pedagogical perspective with participatory activities meant to enable transformative learning (Mezirow, 2000, 2008). Specific steps were taken to enable learning and to overcome potential barriers to learning. These were based on guiding principles outlined in Sinclair et al. (2009). "Individual presentations, small- and full-group discussions were used to encourage inclusive dialogue and generate, discuss and assess ideas" (p. 3). Those kinds of interactions were designed depending on the particular goal of the activity. For example, small-group discussions (involving all team members from a certain component, e.g., technical component) were often used when establishing guidelines for specific project activities that were to be implemented in all countries; similarly, national teams worked together when deciding how to implement project activities in their specific contexts. When planning and implementing their outreach activities with rural participants, to a greater or lesser extent, university collaborators in all three Central American countries adopted a similar participatory approach.

It is worth describing what the planning process looked like at an international level as the decisions made in these forums guided the implementation of the CIDA project. The process allowed national teams a voice in the planning of the project and the ability to adapt the project to their local contexts. This active participation in the planning process is a very important aspect when assessing the relevance and authenticity of an international development project; moreover, it had a significant impact on the learning that resulted from participation in the project (see Sims 2016 for details). For example, participatory project planning began in Managua in April 2007, primarily involving community-development team members from all four countries. Collaboratively at this workshop we decided what information to collect for the baseline study, what participatory methods to use to gather data, what would be common criteria for community engagement, and initial guiding principles for student practicums. We also developed common criteria to help identify which rural communities should be invited to participate. Following these discussions, each national team made decisions appropriate for their particular contexts. During this meeting, knowledge and training were shared amongst, and with,

Latin collaborators on a variety of appropriate participatory tools (Geilfus, 1998) that could be used to help understand farm families' reality. We decided how to proceed and established timelines together. Gender issues were intentionally included as part of these discussions.

At this initial meeting, the community-development inter-national team members developed a common methodological framework establishing broad guidelines for objectives and activities. This framework allowed enough flexibility that each national team could make appropriate decisions for their own contexts. Such flexibility is a key aspect when trying to make a development project effective in genuinely responding to local needs and concerns, yet still able to respond to a regional (i.e., Central American) problem. We recognized quickly that all national team members should attend these inter-national meetings to enrich the planning process, to be able to move forward together, and to reduce resistance.

In farming communities, the outreach work done illustrates how the inter-national planning process and the different groups of participants (university collaborators, students, farm families, and other stakeholders) complemented one another. For example, in Managua in April 2007, the community-development team developed a university-level course to prepare interested students from the participating universities who had chosen to do a rural fieldwork practicum as part of their professional formation. This course included training in participatory methods to collect community-based data. After taking the course, these students lived with farm families for up to a month, documenting common agricultural practices and particularly focusing on pesticide handling, storage, and use. Over the first three years of project implementation, students participated in these activities. The information they gathered, combined with surveys done for the baseline study, were fundamental in the planning of technical outreach work (e.g., deciding upon which workshops to do in community or what might be the most appropriate approach and focus for farm-level demonstration/experimental plots) and indicator development. For an overview of the inter-national workshops and what project activities were implemented following these participatory planning meetings, please see Sims (2016, Table 1, p. 6).

Especially at the earlier stages of project activity implementation, these regular inter-national meetings provided opportunities for national teams to share their successes and challenges, in turn allowing us to collectively reflect on how best to implement the next stages of community-based activities.

Throughout the project and at multiple levels, there were numerous occasions to critically reflect on process and practice, to pose and solve problems, to discuss, and to use findings and experience as a guide for planning and implementing next steps. The cross-cultural nature of bringing different perspectives together was beneficial in terms of pushing us in our reflection and in our creative response to problems on the ground. As the contexts were unique and dynamic, yet shared certain commonalities, the planning and implementation process had to be adaptive, flexible, and iterative.

Another example of how the planning process led to collaborative learning and resulted in concrete action in community was addressing the Honduran challenge of improper disposal of used pesticide containers in rural communities. These toxic containers were littered or buried in fields and ditches, thrown in streams and essential water sources, or repurposed as household beverage containers. As the Honduran team worked with communities, they became aware of this challenge to human and environmental health. They brought this question to the inter-national meeting in 2009. Together, we posed problems (What causes this behaviour? What are the impacts?) and suggested solutions (What can be done? What are the enablers and barriers to change?) The Costa Rican team was particularly helpful in sharing their experiences, having faced similar challenges. Following these discussions, the Honduran team designed and built pesticide recycling depots in participating communities with their rural participants. They also did outreach workshops to teach farm families and school children how to dispose of containers safely by triple-washing them to remove all toxic residue. In each of the participating communities, a local community member volunteered to be responsible for the depot. Furthermore, the Honduran team organized with local industry to have the pesticide containers collected for official recycling.

Essential Project-Based Learning Design Elements: Looking at the CIDA Project Through a Project-Based Learning Pedagogical Lens

Larmer et al. (2015) of the Buck Institute outline what they consider the essential elements for project-based learning. In what follows, I will explore how each of these occurred through the CIDA project.

Challenging problems or questions
Wiggins and McTighe (2005) explain how essential questions help focus the learning process. Their aim is to "stimulate thought, to provoke inquiry, and to spark more questions.... Deep and transferable understandings depend upon framing work around such questions" (p. 106). Chiarotto (2011) explains that inquiry-based learning places students' questions and ideas at the centre of learning experiences, so that their questions drive the learning process forward. Students are encouraged to ask and genuinely investigate their own questions about the world. Knowledge problems arise from efforts to understand the world. Specifically, in the context of project-based learning, Larmer et al. (2015) ask: What is the problem to investigate and solve?

In this CIDA project, the overarching problem was to understand which current pesticide handling, storage, and management practices of small-scale farmers in Central America (especially Costa Rica, Honduras, and Nicaragua) led to negative health and environmental impacts. Following data collected through the baseline study and students living in community, we asked the following questions:

- According to the specific cultural and socio-economic contexts, which actions are most appropriate and needed to address and improve the situation (i.e., through educational outreach, through creating infrastructure, through creating policy)?
- How are the different members in a community and within a family affected by inappropriate pesticide use and handling (e.g., men through applying pesticides with no protective gear, women washing the clothes, children helping in the fields)?
- How can we best reach and educate these members of the community? What interventions should be targeted for which groups?
- What roles can other actors/stakeholders play to enable a transition to alternative-to-chemical practices and safer pesticide use (i.e., university collaborators, government organizations, pesticide-distributor companies, market intermediaries, consumers)?

Sustained inquiry
To inquire is to investigate – it takes time. It is an iterative process where learners are asking deeper and deeper questions in searching for solutions. Different

"sources" can be consulted and incorporated, such as doing traditional research through literature, and doing field-based interviews involving experts, service-providers, and users (Larmer et al., 2015). Within an inquiry-based learning process, teachers facilitate students' learning by providing skills, resources, and experiences that enable learners to investigate, reflect, and rigorously discuss potential solutions. The learning approach must be responsive and flexible (Chiarotto, 2011; Kozak & Elliot, 2014).

This CIDA project, at its heart, was a process of inquiry. From the initial conception of the project, questions around what, why, and how small-scale farm families were producing food and working the land, particularly focusing on how they were interacting and using pesticides, were constantly being asked and investigated. The inter-national planning meetings amongst the national teams allowed project collaborators to share information and knowledge. Through this sharing of information, we were able to learn about the different contexts that gave them a greater understanding of the regional reality. Critical discussion amongst team members, through problem-posing and problem-solving activities, pushed us in our thinking, allowed us to learn and share with one another, and allowed us to plan project activities most appropriate for our individual local contexts. These were then implemented and project successes and challenges revisited at the next inter-national planning meeting. This iterative process continued throughout the six years of the project. The process was time-consuming, but extremely rich in terms of learning results.

The breadth of experience of the people involved in the CIDA project greatly enriched our knowledge base, the inquiry process, and our possibility of learning from one another. We were all educators. The university teams consisted of academics, experts in their fields from four countries. These experts included soil scientists, entomologists, social workers, agronomists, resource managers, agro-economists, and educators, to name but a few. These professional fields of expertise were complemented by farmers' knowledge of their land, their communities, and their farming systems. Local government ministries and technicians were also involved. Students who did rural practicums gained extremely valuable experience and knowledge in understanding how and why farmers farm the way they do. Moreover, student involvement was important in educating them to be more responsible and accountable as future professionals with respect to the environment and to farmers' needs and reality (often agricultural students end up working in rural communities selling agro-chemicals for local distributors). Local industries were also involved in promoting the recycling of containers and the safer practices of using appropriate protective gear and appropriate dosage.

Authenticity

Authenticity generally means that something is real, not fake. Larmer et al. (2015) explain that project-based learning can be authentic in context and can have a real impact on others in addressing a problem. Project-based learning can have personal authenticity in speaking to learners' own concerns, interests, and issues in their lives. When learning is considered authentic, it increases learners' motivation. Chiarotto (2011) and Kozak and Elliot (2014) affirm the value, within an environmental inquiry-based approach, of exploring authentic questions.

I would consider this CIDA project authentic as it aimed to address a concern shared by farmers and the broader society alike. Farm families and community organizations in all contexts expressed concerns about negative health and environmental effects as a result of inappropriate pesticide use and handling (e.g., skin rashes, poisonings, empty pesticide containers being re-used as household beverage containers, high levels of miscarriages for pregnant women who had applied pesticides to their crops using no protective gear, food being sold in the market having high levels of pesticide residue). For academics, this project allowed team members to help address an acute need in their communities and provided an opportunity for them to do research. Funding for opportunities to do practical community-based research are rare in Central American universities. This opportunity for professional development combined with community development, as well as the chance to make decisions for their own contexts, was greatly appreciated by all national team members.

Student voice and choice

Larmer et al. (2015) describe the importance of learners having a say in a project because it creates a sense of ownership. They describe how, in project-based learning, students have control over certain aspects of the project, from the questions they generate, to the resources they use to find answers, to the roles and tasks of team members, to the products they create. At the outset of this chapter, this element of the importance of learners' voice in planning and decision making is explored and contextualized as it relates to international development and natural resources and environmental management literature (Diduck et al., 2012; Sims, 2012, 2016).

Within the CIDA project, participants had a voice in project activities and focus in a variety of ways. They controlled their own resources. Indeed, "communal participation in the generation of knowledge allowed for collective values and needs to influence project activities. This allowed for the project to be sensitive to individual national and community contexts yet relevant regionally, and for the project to be constructed together" (Sims, 2016, p. 14).

Reflection

Reflection is an essential element of project-based learning. Larmer et al. (2015) describe how learners should reflect on what, how, and why they are learning throughout a project. This reflection can occur in a variety of forums. It can focus on content knowledge, on the success of skill development, and on the project itself, in order to potentially improve a next project. Chiarotto (2011) affirms the importance of reflective critical discourse in an inquiry-based learning process.

In this CIDA project, critical reflection, enabled within a supportive learning environment, was an essential part of the learning process (Mezirow, 2000, 2008). In Sims (2016), the learning results from participation in the project and the activities that enabled that learning to occur are explored:

> Structured pedagogical activities and the intent to create the ideal conditions for learning at the inter-national planning level as well as in other project activities enabled a supportive learning environment and more equitable relationships between university collaborators and other participants. Rational discourse enabled participants to reflect critically on their own assumptions, regional challenges, opportunities, and pest management practices. Deliberative learning forums included facilitated dialogical processes and hands-on, practical methods; the latter particularly with farmers. The design and implementation of the CIDA project encouraged participants to explore new patterns of behaviour, then, through regular meetings at a communal, national, and inter-national level, to critically reflect as to the efficacy of their actions as a guide for next steps. This continual cycle of actions based on reflection, framed by concerns for human health and environmental protection, led to transformative learning and praxis.... An interdisciplinary approach

exposed professionals to diverse perspectives and to the multi-faceted nature of this problem pushing them to think more broadly and deeply. An appreciation for the gendered division of farm-related tasks, and of men and women as part of project teams, enabled them to more adequately address a complex issue.

Structured activities that promoted significant learning outcomes were working collaboratively to: plan and implement project activities, experiment with alternative pest management techniques on demonstration plots, participate in workshop-style outreach activities, and for students to live with farm families... [A]ll of these forums provided room for reflection as the process combined participants' experiential knowledge, dialogue, analysis, and abstract conceptualization. Participants put theory into practice and had their practice enriched by learning theory. (Sims, 2016, p.14)

Critique and revision
With a project-based learning approach, providing constructive feedback on students' work is important. Outside adults can contribute to the critique process (Larmer et al., 2015).

In terms of providing constructive feedback on the CIDA project as a whole, mid-term and final reports were helpful to identify successes and challenges. At a farm level, nature gave feedback on the success of the practices promoted in the demonstration plots (e.g., soil samples indicated if the soil was of higher quality; yields indicated whether crops were more bountiful as a result of interventions; farmers saw economic benefit of adopting new greener practices). Farmer uptake of new practices showed project team members if their interventions were relevant and helpful to participants. Project planning meetings, at a national and inter-national level, provided numerous opportunities for team members to reflect upon the efficacy of project activities.

Public product
Within project-based learning, Larmer et al. (2015) argue that sharing learning results in a formalized way with the public makes students take it more seriously; by sharing the results with a broader public, it makes them a point of contemplation, in turn creating a learning community. Making project results public can also be a celebration of students' learning, showing what students are capable of.

Within the CIDA project, at the beginning, the sharing of results made us more accountable to one another, keeping us on task during our already busy professional lives. During the inter-national meetings, often in the country where the meetings were taking place, we visited the farm-demonstration plots to see what kind of work was being done. This was another opportunity to showcase local farmer and technical-team work. The final symposium (Montelimar, Nicaragua, 02/13), which involved project participants from all countries – farmers, university collaborators, students, government ministry collaborators – was a very tangible "public" sharing of learning experiences. It created a learning community that brought together participants from the different nationalities in many ways and levels. Finally, sharing CIDA project results at academic conferences and in publishing peer-reviewed articles has shown the international community what has been done through this project.

Discussion: Similarities and Distinctions between Project-Based Learning in a Classroom Context and in an International-Development Context

When considering project-based learning with adult learners in a development context, the importance of creating meaningful, honest relationships cannot be overstated. This is particularly important in development contexts, as the risks to farmer livelihoods are real when interventions and changes are proposed to the way in which they earn their living. If their crops fail or are less productive, their children might not go to school and families might not eat or be able to purchase medicines. Farmers must trust what the technicians say and the technicians must understand the level of responsibility when proposing changes. Another consideration is that, when there is trust and good relationships, the planning process is easier and discussions are richer. More knowledge is shared. Mediating conflict takes up time and resources. However, a concern with building these relationships is that often the project ends when the funding ends, and the rural participants find it especially hard to understand why there is no longer ongoing communication with people they have become quite close to. This is exacerbated in isolated communities with no phone or internet access, making beyond-project communication even more difficult. For me at least, this (essential) ending of relationships poses some real ethical questions.

In engaging in a process of sustained inquiry in a classroom, students can move on to the next project of interest when the immediate project and its driving question have finished. With this real-life example, the problem persists, just as the challenges and questions facing farmers remain unresolved. We might have moved forward, but the situation has by no means been resolved. The farmers cannot simply contemplate another driving question; their life is food production, and finding ways to produce food and earn a living safely and sustainably is a life-long project.

No matter the context of project-based learning, there are many "teachers" and many "learners." Notwithstanding, after working with adults over six years, I would argue that the amount of knowledge and life experiences that are genuinely shared and created with one another are probably greater than might be found in a classroom context with children. This is particularly true if the professional project teams are interdisciplinary and if all have a deep appreciation for the value of local knowledge and the gifts that all participants bring to the learning forum.

Evaluation in both contexts is ongoing; however, it potentially occurs differently in this real-life example. It is the participants and the environment that provide feedback to the university collaborators in a variety of ways; they can determine whether this project was authentic and responded to their needs, and if the interventions were worth adopting. Because of cultural protocols, constructive "critique" might be subtle (as in, not explicitly verbalized). For example, farmers might participate in a workshop and then either adopt, or not, the recommended practice, depending on how useful they found the information and how realistic it was for them to put it into practice. Specifically, workshops might focus on wearing protective gear when applying pesticides or washing the men's clothes separately from the rest of the families' clothes while wearing a protective plastic apron and gloves. Rural participants might find this information relevant; however, the cost of protective gear, a perception that wearing protective clothing is not *macho*, a tropical climate, and limited access to water might limit a participant's ability or desire to put these ideas into practice.

As in classroom project-based learning, where activities, resources, and approaches are designed around the learners' level, abilities, and interests, this real-life example also tailored its pedagogy to meet the needs of the participants involved. Learners in the CIDA project were a varied group: academics, university students, farm families, technicians, and rural school children. Depending on the learning goals and on the culture and livelihood characteristics of the learners, the activities were tailored to best respond to their needs. For example, as university collaborators, we shared our ongoing results with each other in the planning meetings, often via semiformal presentations. However, with farmers, outreach activities had to be practical, hands-on, and experiential, with results that were clearly evident. By experimenting with alternative pest management and farming techniques on demonstration plots, like vermi-composting, intercropping, and using green cover crop, farmers observed an improvement in soil quality and crop yield. Planting fruit trees helped reduce erosion and increased food security by providing alternative food sources and economic opportunities.

Conclusion

In conclusion, it is easy to see that this particular international development project shares many characteristics with project-based learning in a formal learning context. At the outset of this chapter, I described how an underlying intent of project-based learning is for learners to be able to apply what they have learned to situations in their lives. This exploration of ideas clarifies how taking a project-based learning approach when designing and implementing an international development project could be valuable, as it could help provide participants (i.e., learners) with competencies that allow them to more adequately face enduring challenges.

However, for me a most important distinction is that, in this Central American example, the context is real life, and the problem is a genuine one that affects participants' health and the environment. Interventions have direct impact on participants' lives, particularly on the farm families who are the most vulnerable participants. These participants are directly affected by the success or failure of the proposed solutions; they are the ones taking the risks by changing livelihood practices. As for the Central American university collaborators, they were the ones in the fields with the farmers on an ongoing basis for years. For them, it is not a learning activity that they can easily walk away from; it is one they are deeply invested in.

References

Chiarotto, L. (2011). Natural curiosity: Building children's understanding of the world through environmental inquiry / A resource for teachers. Toronto, ON: The Laboratory School at The Dr. Eric Jackman Institute of Child Study, Ontario Institute for Studies in Education, University of Toronto. *Natural Curiosity: A Resource for Teachers*. Retrieved from http://naturalcuriosity.ca/aboutus.php?m=b

Chibi, A. (2011). Contributions of university partnerships in cooperation and development (UPCD): Tier 2 projects to marginalized populations. Ottawa, ON: Association of Universities and Colleges Canada.

Diduck, A.P., Sinclair, A.J., Hostetler, G., & Fitzpatrick, P. (2012). Transformative learning theory, public involvement and natural resource and environmental management. *Journal of Environmental Planning and Management, 55* (10), 1311-1330.

Geilfus, F. (1998). 80 herramientos para el desarrollo participativo: Diagnóstico, planificación, monitoreo, evaluación. [80 tools for participatory development: Diagnostic, planning, monitoring, evaluation]. El Salvador: IICA Holanda/LADERAS.

Kovak, S., & Elliot, S. (2011). Connecting the dots: Key strategies that transform learning for environmental education, citizenship and sustainability. *Learning for a Sustainable Future (LSF)*. Retrieved from lsf-lst.ca

Larmer, J., Mergendoller, J., & Boss, S. (2015). Setting the standard for project based learning: A proven approach to rigorous classroom instruction. Alexandria, VA: ASCD.

Mezirow, J. (2000). Learning to think like an adult: Core concepts of transformative theory. In J. Mezirow & Associates (Eds.), *Learning as transformation* (pp. 3-34). San Francisco, CA: Jossey-Bass.

Mezirow, J. (2008). An overview on transformative learning. In P. Sutherland & J. Crowther (Eds.), *Lifelong learning: Concepts and contexts* (pp. 24-37). London: Routledge.

Mulock, B., & Herrera, J. (2013). Community-based pest management in Central American agriculture final narrative report. Ottawa, ON: Association of Universities and Colleges Canada.

Sims, L. (2012). Taking a learning approach to community-based strategic environmental assessment: Results from a Costa Rican case study. *Impact Assessment and Project Appraisal, 30*, 242-252.

Sims, L. (2016). Learning for sustainability through CIDA's "Community-based pest management in Central American agriculture" project: A deliberative, experiential and iterative process. *Journal of Environmental Planning and Management.* http://dx.doi.org/10.1080/09640568.2016.1165188

Sinclair, A.J., Sims, L., & Spaling, H. (2009). Community-based approaches to strategic environmental assessment: Lessons from Costa Rica. *Environmental Impact Assessment Review, 29*, 147-156.

Spaling, H., Montes, J., & Sinclair, A.J. (2011). Best practices for promoting participation and learning from community-based environmental assessment in Kenya and Tanzania. *Journal of Environmental Assessment, Policy and Management, 13,* 343-366.

Wiggins, G., & McTighe, J. (2005). *Understanding by design* (2nd ed.). Alexandria, VA: Association for Supervision and Curriculum Development.

About the Authors
Jonathan Dueck teared up a little when watching the movie Home with his family. He knows at least three jokes that he shares relentlessly with his students. Once, when he was five, he tried to bungee jump out of the maple tree in his front yard. He has been taking small risks ever since, learning from each mistake along the way.
Keith Fulford has had a pet. During nonteaching hours he likes the jokes. Keith has a history of using author bio advice websites. He takes joy in the work and creativity of working as an educator.

Who Should Read This Chapter?
Inventors. Hopeful educators. Wizards in training. Humorists.

The Theme of This Chapter in Three Words
Heart, body, mind.

As Educators, What Are You Passionate About?
Constructivist-psychedelic-pedagogical anarchism with a dash of Gramsci.
Social learning.

CHAPTER 6

How Can Projects Work for Our Most Vulnerable Learners?

Keith Fulford and Jonathan Dueck, Argyle School
Winnipeg, Manitoba, Canada

The art and science of education can involve an obscure world. The certainty of learning outcomes, rubrics, and lesson plans can offer linear clarity, but the uncertainty of student experience, readiness, and cognitive patterns can impose chaos. In between these moments of clarity and chaos, we find the spirit of learning. The spirit of learning is felt with mind, heart, and body. It is assembled by learners as they share part of themselves with the world. We start from the position that an underserved learner will often see a greater distance between their self and the world. The work of education is to have each student see their self as *part* of the world.

We believe that an education experience for underserved learners must shock their system. We have written this document in a manner that embraces the space between certainty and chaos. We ask you to be open and take this document in that spirit. Within the spaces of this document, you will find your place in the PBL world.

It is in that space that you will actively choose to assemble your work as a PBL educator.

At times, what you read will not feel like writing you might expect to find in a book like this, but we are inviting you to build relationships. Relationships are work. Relationships require participation. Relationships create new spaces. We cannot explain to you what that space is – we have to *live* it.

Introduction

Our learning is an expression of life lived with our heart, body, and mind. In our practice we approach our work with students by believing that:

- Learning with our heart means building personal connections and relationships.
- Learning with our body means building products to be touched and exchanged.
- Learning with our mind means building descriptions and labels.

Our happiness in our community is built around the world we experience using these three parts. Our PBL classroom asks students to live in their learning by connecting with their heart, body, and mind.

We know our student is not unlike students found in schools everywhere: a student who is seemingly resistant to school experiences and who is often set in habits and attitudes that degrade, sabotage, and interfere with a learning opportunity. The contributing factors to our underserved student's attitude usually include trauma, abuse, and brain differences.

Underserved learners will exhibit habits of chronic absenteeism and "behavioural" issues ranging from oppositional defiance to attention deficit and other "anti-social" behaviour. This observation in a classroom, in our opinion, is linked to an underserved student's way of thinking. Underserved students may be rigid, inward-looking, and fatalistic. They are often afflicted by this habit of mind – a way of thinking that restricts engagement and relationship.

We use PBL because it gives us the best opportunity to engage each other in a classroom that learns in relationship with our head, heart, and body. We have represented these three parts with images throughout this chapter to outline how our pedagogy is truly a continuum of learning: a process of relationship-building and knowledge construction.

In our PBL classroom we use:

Authentic experience and assessment to activate the mind in a way that counteracts fatalistic thinking.

Action and self-efficacy to activate the body in a way that focuses attention outward.

♡ Community and shared artifacts to activate the heart in a way that counteracts rigidity.

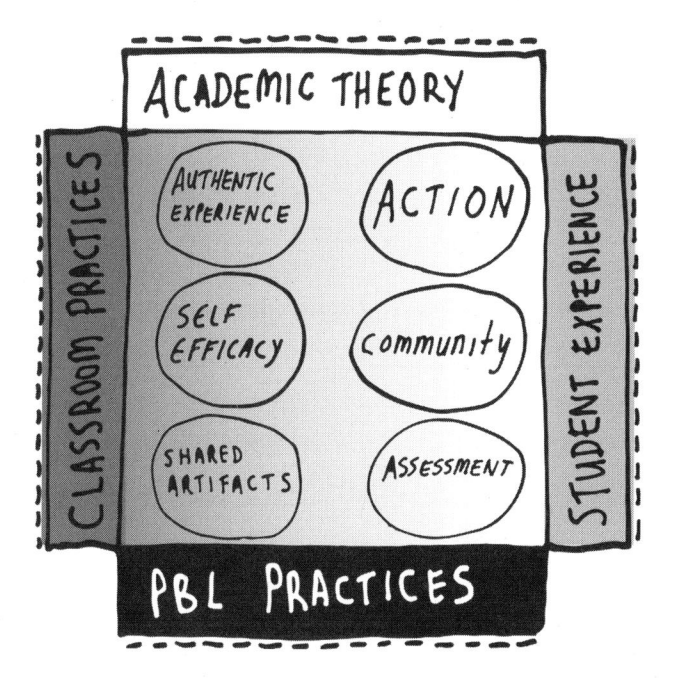

ACADEMIC THEORY

CLASSROOM PRACTICES | STUDENT EXPERIENCE

- Authentic Experience
- Action
- Self Efficacy
- Community
- Shared Artifacts
- Assessment

PBL PRACTICES

At the end of each section, to assist in describing our approach, we have referenced the relevant component of the essential project design elements of PBL from the Buck Institute for Education (Larmer, J., Boss, S., & Mergendoller, J., 2015). The essential project design elements state that project-based learning requires the use of sustained inquiry, authenticity, student voice and choice, reflection, critique and revision, public product, and challenging problem or question (Larmer et al., 2015). Inserted components are not meant to be prescriptive. The connection is meant to highlight the process and thinking we have used in our project-based learning practice with our student population.

We have inserted student voices to complement and explain content in each section. You will notice that an italic font is used to signal that a student voice is being shared. These quotes are actual responses to questions formed to gather information about students describing their experience of each section. The way they are inserted into the text is not arbitrary, but relates directly to the nearby writing. The reader is invited to build relationships between the quotes and the text.

Authentic Product

For an underserved student, we believe that the mind needs to be engaged toward others to activate learning. The 1989 film *Field of Dreams* gave us a piece of false wisdom: "If you build it, he will come" (Gordon et al., 1989). Building rarely occurs before an audience is present. Before audiences there could be experimenting, doodling, fiddling, playing, and messing around. While all of these are important activities for preparing ourselves to create, it isn't until an audience has been identified that meaning can start to take shape and the process of learning can begin. Pablo Helguera says in his book *Education for Socially Engaged Art* that "we build *because* audiences exist. We build because we seek to reach out to others" (p. 22).

> *To change something or to make something, you have to actually know what you want* (student discussion, personal conversation, June 9, 2017).

In a classroom setting, when the student builds with other humans in mind, they are placing content and knowledge into context. The student is "making sense" of information, overcoming a fatalistic way of thinking, and moving toward recognizing that their skills and knowledge are important to others.

When working from a PBL model, the student might be building to present to a professional in the field, or to offer solutions to actual problems in their community. In either case, the student must analyze and apply the information gathered about a topic and situate it in a real-world context. Students need to ask themselves, "What would a graphic designer be looking for in a successful poster design?" or "How can I meet the needs of specific community members through my work?"

> *When you are showing for the public, then you have to know the answer and not rely on other people to know* (student discussion, personal conversation, June 9, 2017).

When the student builds with an audience in mind, it gives purpose to their thinking. The student begins to describe why they are using the information that they are and how it might be received by their chosen audience.

> *It was all the stress that was put on me personally while building it that kinda made me want to learn* (student discussion, personal conversation, June 9, 2017).

In doing so the student will not only grow in their understanding, but will build empathy toward others and change their own fatalistic way of thinking. What the student is building matters to others because he or she has considered them first.

> *Knowing what 'great' looks like!* (student discussion, personal conversation, June 9, 2017).

Our classroom regularly invited community members and professionals to join us in making our learning. Graphic designers gave feedback on poster designs and assessed how well they communicated the desired message; a filmmaker shared his experience with climate change and people living in northern Canada; and local community activists shared about challenges residents have around food security.

> *It felt kinda cool to get a professional person to help me with a poster. It's kinda like when you go to the gym and you get a personal trainer* (student discussion, personal conversation, June 9, 2017).

Our final project for the year asked students to imagine what the barriers at Portage and Main might look like today if Indigenous people and immigrants had been able to use the concept of placemaking to build a community together 200 years ago. The resulting models were displayed in a very public place near the school, and each student was required to be present and field any questions that visitors might have about the display. Engaging in authentic learning and creating public products counteracted fatalistic thinking because the student had to consider others in their work and expect feedback from the public. Accepting that role and performing within it is an act of growth. The student engaging in project-based learning accepts change and development. These experiences oppose fatalistic thinking.

> *It felt like a little bit more than a school project. It felt like something I was genuinely interested in. It felt like it was more than marks and getting a credit* (student discussion, personal conversation, June 9, 2017).

We relate this section on authentic product to the essential project design elements of PBL because the student produced a public product and engaged in authentic learning.

Assessment

Imagine the experience of a student who has a history of clinical appointments. The term *assessment* sets the conditions for high anxiety. Assessment is a thing that is "done to" the student. The underserved student will often experience such scrutiny with a fatalistic way of thinking.

> *In my other schools, teachers just wanted me to pass – but this was different, you guys really wanted me to understand* (student discussion, personal conversation, June 9, 2017).

Our planning and approach is to imagine assessment as part of our classroom narrative; it is not an event but a way of doing. In our PBL classroom, we attempt to experience assessment as a way to live and exchange ideas. Assessment provides coherence through a year of different projects. Our approach to assessment as a component of PBL engages the mind to counteract fatalistic thinking.

> *We are able to explain to substitutes what we were doing* (student discussion, personal conversation, June 9, 2017).

Assessment is embedded in the idea of growth as well as the purposeful reliance on the idea that action-and-response is a personal power to be practised and refined. Assessment is the refinement our classroom relies upon to explain relevance and application.

We practice the experience of labelling and responding daily. The Wheel of Feel was an opportunity to label mood and attitude. This student-created system equated mood and attitude descriptors to colours on a colour wheel. At the beginning of every class, each student was asked to label how they felt based on this system. The responses were recorded in a data collection chart designed by each student.

This daily routine was an initiation into a practice of gathering specific data or concepts, processing the information, and attempting to apply that information to our classroom problem.

Project-based learning is a framework that allows for planning and classroom approaches to engage the minds of students struggling within fatalistic thinking.

We relate this section on assessment to the essential project design elements of PBL because the student was engaging in critique and revision.

Action

For an underserved student, we believe that the body needs to be employed to activate learning. Learning by doing is a timeless education strategy, found in informal sayings such as "trial by fire" and structured concepts such as apprenticeships. Engaging the body physically shifts inward ways of thinking outward.

> *It felt like I got to take the wheel on my learning* (student discussion, personal conversation, June 9, 2017).

We plan to immerse our students in the physical experience of learning.

> *The physical shape of the classroom – it felt like we were in a meeting – we were expected to give feedback* (student discussion, personal conversation, June 9, 2017).

We initiate the school year by participating in an international urban guerrilla activism event called "PARK(ing) Day" (https://www.parkingday.org/about-parking-day). The event challenges participants to redesign on-street parking spaces to welcome people and pedestrians.

> *We went out to visit the place* (student discussion, personal conversation, June 9, 2017).

Through the experience of creating an entertaining and often absurd PARK(ing) Day exhibit, we're able to involve our students in learning core classroom concepts around use of space, use of materials, and design process. The event offers our students the ability to connect, make, and find success early. Quickly, students begin to accept the initiating stage of learning by using a class mantra: "Energy yes, quality no" (Art21.org, 2014).

Project-based learning requires planning and practice that relies on action. It's the use of the body that can redirect an underserved learner from inward-thinking habits to outward-thinking habits.

We relate action to the essential project design elements of PBL because students faced a challenging problem in an authentic environment.

Self-Efficacy

We believe the destructive ways of thinking in an underserved student can be addressed by engaging the body. We use physical experience to revise our student's belief in their capability to organize and execute the courses of action required to manage prospective situations. Our students can come from a wide range of experiences. They join our school usually as a result of a stressor, often an inability (as the definition of self-efficacy states) to organize and execute the courses of action required to manage prospective situations. We are a school "of choice" – often the only choice. We believe this is the exact moment for PBL. We believe our classroom should offer an opportunity for this underserved student to engage in imaging and producing their learning experience through a sense of self-efficacy. We aim to counteract the cycle of inward-looking thinking by engaging the body.

> *Before that I wasn't really involved in school at all – but being in that classroom made me feel really empowered – it made me feel like I was smart enough to be in school – that I could do school* (student discussion, personal conversation, June 9, 2017).

We use PBL as a series of moments for the student to feel learning – that it is the engagement of the body that can support them in developing familiarity and mastery of complex content and analysis.

> *I knew I had to be confident, I had to know what decisions I made...*
> (student discussion, personal conversation, June 9, 2017).

Specifically, we take the opportunity for the student to develop an academic self-efficacy. We rely on a method of analysis that allows our classroom community to maintain a curious approach. We find that the act of curiosity is the necessary starting point for the student to live with a belief in their capability to organize and execute the courses of action required to manage prospective situations.

We conference with our students regularly to provide opportunities for them to continue to label and control their own learning experiences.

> *You can't rely on others to know the answers* (student discussion, personal conversation, June 9, 2017).

The cycle of our design process provides a coherent tool for our students to manage their classroom experience. This tool is personalized by the student. It is important to have the student personalize their design process by identifying stage, actions, and results. For example, the starting point of a design process may be "discovery." The student would have to identify the definition of discovery in the context of design, be exposed to tools to use when in that stage, and, lastly, determine what results to expect when that stage is complete. Additionally, we reference the stages of learning to calm the experience of acquiring and developing knowledge (Adams, 2016):

- You don't know you don't know
- You know you don't know
- You know you know
- You don't know you know

The acknowledgment of this cognitive path of learning, along with project design, eases our students and shows them a path of relationship. Amid the chaos, a repetition of the process shines a light on the direction of learning.

> *If I had a rough day, I told the class about it.... It was really cool, you would relate it back to the stages of learning, and you would say if you don't go back and fix things it is difficult to have something to be proud of* (student discussion, personal conversation, June 9, 2017).

Project-based learning allows our learner to engage the body as learning, and to experience and recognize learning as theirs to organize and produce. We aim to promote self-efficacy to counteract an underserved student's inward thinking.

> *I got to control what I was learning* (student discussion, personal conversation, June 9, 2017).

This section on self-efficacy relates to the essential project-design elements of PBL, because the student had voice and choice and was engaged in sustained inquiry.

Community

With an underserved student, we believe that the heart needs to be engaged to counteract rigidity in learning. One way to do this is to encourage the development of a shared "language." For example, between the years of 1996 and 2008, a small group of artists and friends met on a weekly basis in Winnipeg, Manitoba, to create. They called themselves the Royal Art Lodge. The output of their exhibited work included collaborative drawings, paintings, videos, costumes, dolls, comics, and audio recordings. The name conjures up a wide array of different fraternal order groups like the Elks Lodge, the Shriners, the Freemasons, or even (maybe most appropriately) the Loyal Order of Water Buffaloes (of which Barney Rubble and Fred Flintstone are members). There is an aura of mystery surrounding all of these groups, which is reinforced by secret passwords, rituals, oaths, regalia, and symbolism.

> *I think the difference is that I came out of that class...I feel like...*
> *it's not just like a carton of milk pouring into a mind bowl or something*
> (student discussion, personal conversation, June 9, 2017).

The collection of these shared and "secret" experiences creates a language system that is unique to the group and helps to unite and strengthen its members in relation to community.

> *It helped us connect together. It made us want to engage with the learning*
> *and the work* (student discussion, personal conversation, June 9, 2017).

This shared language is central to the development of a familiar space where much more is possible. Working as a community gives each student a security that can soften their rigidity and lead to a kind of creative risk-taking that just isn't possible when they work alone.

> *It was true that we were all like gears working together*
> (student discussion, personal conversation, June 9, 2017).

We often think of communities like this in terms of two different TV shows we each watched as a child: Voltron and Power Rangers. In both cases, individuals who had unique powers would unite and form a super-robot through which their powers combined into an unstoppable force. When the Power Rangers needed to unite, they'd yell, "It's morphin' time!"

The task as an educator is to patiently find a way to "morph" a collection of diverse individuals into a community of learners that is better together than apart.

As a class we had a few different rituals that happened daily, weekly, or otherwise. Projects like the aforementioned "Wheel of Feel" helped to ground the students and prepare them to learn. This process created comfort in being vulnerable and worked toward softening hard hearts.

> *Laughter is a big part of creating community. In order to move ahead as a community, you have to learn to laugh together* (student discussion, personal conversation, June 9, 2017).

During our time together, we also shared humour, absurdity, and inside jokes to create a comfortable and less-threatening environment for learning. Students often began the class feeling disoriented and lost, but ended our time together feeling connected with others.

We relate this section on community to the essential project design elements of PBL because the student had voice and choice and could work in a community that was safe for reflection.

Shared Artifacts

With an underserved student, we believe that the heart needs to be shared with others in order to overcome a rigid attitude toward learning. Francis Alÿs is a Belgian-born artist who relocated to Mexico City in 1986 and has been based there ever since. He is best known for his seemingly absurd actions that are carefully planned and concise. In *The Collectors* (1990–92), Alÿs created a group of small magnetized sculptures on wheels that resembled children's toys shaped like dogs. He took these "dogs" on walks through the streets of Mexico City and, because they were magnetized, the dogs collected any discarded metallic material lying on the street. These dogs with their collections served as tokens of particular streets in a specific city.

A token is a physical object that exists to represent or stand in place of a quality, feeling, experience, fact, place, event, and so on. Tokens help us to remember people, events, and certain time frames in our lives. As humans we do this very often. Bringing home souvenirs from a trip helps us to remember that place in a certain way. Religious groups create tokens in objects, images, and rituals to help their adherents remember important teachings.

> *Like when you came back with those papers soaked in lemon juice* (student discussion, personal conversation, June 9, 2017).

Creating "tokens" in a classroom environment is a useful way to offload specific learning onto products created through the learning process. These products transform from *expressions* of knowledge into *bestowers* of knowledge. When the student is asked to share in creating these artifacts with others, it builds trust between individuals. The sharing of memories builds community.

> *Oh, those masks! Ya, it's coming back to me...the video*
> (student discussion, personal conversation, June 9, 2017).

PBL offers this opportunity because each artifact produced by a learner contains the memory of building knowledge about a certain topic or concept. The student can look at the poster or model they created and be reminded of what understandings those objects stand for. Products of learning become props where learning can be stored to empower thought and make space for even more complex forms. They can also stand for shared experiences in the classroom and work to build relationships among others. Each student shared their learning along with others in a visible, physical form for all to see.

> *I learned how good it felt to have a finished product in my hand*
> (student discussion, personal conversation, June 9, 2017).

In our classroom, the students created interview videos while wearing masks of a prominent visual artist; constructed a "text-book" illustrating the student's version of the design process; held papers that simulated ancient texts; built an actual "thinking cap"; produced animations that illustrated change over time; made city-council superpower trading cards; , and much more. These artifacts were not content knowledge for our learners, but the way in which students could reference, relate, and explain content knowledge. Each of these products was in a moment connected to the content that informed our final exhibit. In designing and using these artifacts, students reinforced content knowledge as well as a commitment to the design process that empowered our project-based learning classroom. When making these shared artifacts, the student was opening their heart to others in the classroom, which opened new opportunities for understanding and relationship.

We relate our section on shared artifacts to the essential project design elements of PBL because the student had to work out a challenging problem that led to further reflection on their learning.

Outro

We find with our learners that school is a highly cognitive and mind-based experience. For an underserved learner, the result is a restrictive way of thinking. This way of thinking is inward-looking, rigid, and fatalistic. The underserved learner will be trapped in this pattern of a cognitive-mind-dominant experience. In our practice, PBL is a framework plan for engaging the mind, body, and heart of our learners.

We believe a PBL classroom offers the most opportunity to separate the student from their restrictive habits of mind by engaging the heart, body, and mind. For the student it's the framework for moving from being a rigid, inward-looking, and fatalistic thinker to being a learner who feels he or she *does*:

- Build personal connections and relationships.
- Build products to be touched and exchanged.
- Build descriptions and labels.

PBL is a method for the underserved learner to feel they are part of a world that has often been distant. It involves being open to making choices, carrying out actions, and building relationships in the space between clarity and chaos. We believe that embracing that space by using the framework above is the model for practicing PBL with underserved learners.

References

Adams, L. (2016). *Learning a new skill is easier said than done.* Retrieved from http://www.gordontraining.com/free-workplace-articles/learning-a-new-skill-is-easier-said-than-done/#

art21. (2014, October 24). Thomas Hirschhorn in "Investigation" [Season 7, video file]. *Art in the Twenty-First Century.* Retrieved from https://art21.org/watch/art-in-the-twenty-first-century/s7/thomas-hirschhorn-in-investigation-segment/

Bandura, A. (2002). *Social learning theory.* Englewood Cliffs, NJ: Prentice-Hall.

Butler, I. (2011, June 28). Are you…Can you…Were you? (Felt) [Recorded by Shabazz Palaces]. *Black Up* [album]. Seattle, WA: Sub Pop.

Gordon, L., & Gordon, C. (Producers), & Robinson, P. A. (Director). (1989). *Field of dreams* [Motion picture on DVD]. United States: Universal Pictures.

Helguera, P. (2011). *Education for socially engaged art: A materials and techniques handbook.* New York, NY: Jorge Pinto Books.

Larmer, J., Boss, S., & Mergendoller, J. (2015). Gold standard PBL: Essential project design elements. Alexandria, VA: ASCD. Retrieved from http://www.bie.org/bloggold_standard_pbl_essential_project_design_elements

About the Author
Matt Henderson is Assistant Superintendent of Seven Oaks School Division and former principal (and teacher) at the Maples Met School, a Big Picture Learning School located within the Seven Oaks School Division. He loves working with kids on projects and is always blown away by how much he learns from learners each and every day. Matt has been exploring project-based learning for over a decade, specifically within the spheres of experience and ecological literacy. He completed his master's degree in 2016 and is currently pursuing his PhD at the University of Manitoba.

Who Should Read This Chapter?
Educators who wish to engage in how the K–12 system might support all learners.

The Theme of This Chapter in Three Words
Autism. Inclusion. Celebration.

As an Educator, What Are You Passionate About?
I am passionate about doing projects. I am passionate about tapping into the curiosity of learners and fostering educative environments for learners and educators that are based on trust, inquiry, and exploring our purpose on this planet.

CHAPTER 7

How Can Project-Based Learning Work with Learners on the Autism Spectrum?

Matt Henderson, Seven Oaks School Division and Maples Met School
Winnipeg, Manitoba, Canada

In the Beginning

For many of us of a certain generation, our first interaction with this thing called autism was Dustin Hoffman's 1988 characterization in the film *Rain Man*. In the film, Hoffman plays the role of Raymond Babbitt, an autistic man who displays incredibly narrow interests, an astounding memory, savant-like math skills, and several other idiosyncrasies. At the time, this character created an incredible amount of disequilibrium for me and many within our society. What was this thing called autism? Is this how it manifested itself in all individuals? Was it curable?

While many families had been struggling with autism for decades, *Rain Man* brought it into public view. Since then, school communities have been working hard with families to try and best serve the unique needs of learners on the autism spectrum. Champions like Temple Grandin have been tremendous advocates for those with Autism Spectrum Disorder (ASD). Research seems to be closer to the causes and best strategies for fully realizing the potential of ASD learners, while also educating those of us in the mainstream who often seek to condemn behaviours and perspectives that we deem abnormal.

In my early teaching career, in what seems like a former life, students on the autism spectrum were part of my learning communities. Unfortunately, I was too ill-equipped and lacked courage to properly understand where these learners were coming from. In those days, in most school divisions, students who were perceived to present behavioural challenges for the classroom were sent to the margins of the class, seated exclusively beside an equally ill-equipped educational assistant, and were only included in learning experiences when it was deemed "appropriate." Today I don't feel great about this pseudo-teaching, but I see it as a starting point for moving toward making our schools more inclusive to all students.

Recently, I was asked with a group of other educators to develop a Met School, a project-based and internship-based school based on the Big Picture Learning (BPL) model. Big Picture Schools, or Met Schools[1], are fully learner-based. They are firmly based on the "advisory" model. Every learner is part of an advisory of approximately 15 learners. These learners are together with their one advisor for all four years of their high school career. The advisory works with each learner and their family to design a specific learning plan for that child that is firmly founded on the child's passions. Advisories become families, where learners and advisors look out for each other and build the deep relationships needed for rich and authentic learning.

Big Picture Schools are also firmly based on internships. On Tuesdays and Thursdays, learners head out on their internships, where they work with adults in the field on projects that they are both passionate about. Our learners do adult work that is real and gives back to their organization. Advisors and mentors meet with the learner to develop LTI (Learning Through Internship) goals and to assess how the mentorship is progressing.

Project-based learning is also a key element, but only one part, of the pedagogical framework of Big Picture Learning, at least at the Maples Met School. Learners, in conjunction with their advisors, develop projects based on essential questions they have about the universe. As the learners grow and transform, they are able to propose projects with less and less scaffolding. Part of our proposal process sees learners explore the Manitoba curriculum and select outcomes and competencies that they want to be assessed on, and also outcomes

---

1 The very first Big Picture School was opened in Providence, Rhode Island, two decades ago and was called the Metropolitan Regional Career and Technical Centre. Hence "The Met." Not all Big Picture Schools are called Met Schools, but all Met Schools are Big Picture Learning Schools. At present, there are two Big Picture Learning schools in Canada, and they are both on Jefferson Avenue in Winnipeg: The Seven Oaks Met School and the Maples Met School. For more information, head to www.bigpicture.org.

they need to achieve in order to earn credits. Learners in Manitoba need 30 high school credits to graduate with a diploma.

At the Met, learners are also assessed through public exhibitions. Four times a year, learners are asked to stand up in front of their peers, their mentors, their families, and their advisor to prove what they have learned. Learners are asked to demonstrate not what they have done, but what they have learned. They need to walk us through how they achieved specific outcomes and provide evidence of their learning. Following each exhibition, the learners, advisor, and family sit down and review the learning plan before setting new goals.

BPL is all about what we call "leaving to learn." That is, we're always getting out of the building and heading into the field. We're not beholden to a rigid timetable, so when learners say "I need to talk to this physicist," or "I need to pick up this bracket," or "I need to visit this CSA farm," we're able to just go.

Learners are at the heart of what we do – not timetables, systems, buildings, or the primary needs of adults. Given this leeway, we were all really excited about designing a school with intention that was solely focused on the interests and passion of each individual student. As our slogan is "one student at a time," we were enthusiastic, and perhaps idealistic, about the opportunity to create and foster powerful learning experiences that went deep. Indeed, the past two years have been incredible. Using the experience and passion of learners to allow them to dive deep into what excites them produces profound opportunities for learning and creating meaningful relationships. We've been blown away by the incredible internships the learners have cultivated. These learners and mentors have designed some effective projects with real-world implications. We love coming to work!

Having said this, we were not prepared for the enthusiastic response learners with autism spectrum disorders would have. Roughly 1 percent of the general population is on the autism spectrum, although the data from Canada, the UK, and the US fluctuates. (For example, 1 out of 68 people are diagnosed in Canada versus 1 in 88 in the UK.) What we discovered was that 10 percent of our incoming learners had been diagnosed with autism. We also discovered that we were ultimately clueless about how we should attend to the needs of our learners on the spectrum. We were ignorant even in terms of how we might design the physical space. What we did quickly realize, however, was that these were our learners and we needed to do some action research quickly in order to be able to respond to them.

While I'll speak to the individual stories of our learners later (and in fact they'll speak for themselves), our journey began shortly after we realized our situation. Early in our first year, I was feeling pretty underwhelmed about how we hadn't responded as well as we could have to our learners on the spectrum. (It's always about us, isn't it?). I didn't even know where to begin when I arrived at a monthly administrators' meeting. A colleague of mine, Karen Hiscott, who is a principal at a K-5 school, was giving a presentation on her research at the graduate level on ASD. As she spoke to her findings and her experience, I clung emotionally to her ankles and immediately invited her to speak to our faculty. Naturally, Karen said yes and we began an incredible foray into the subject, involving experts in our school division and our local community who were more than willing to help, guide, challenge, and celebrate our journey. Finding the right support team for your learning community is paramount, and our school community has been blessed by the tremendous enthusiasm for learner success in our division, city, and province.

Our journey began in September 2016 – a journey into how a project-based and student-centred school might indeed live up to its name and ultimately evolve into a fully inclusive community that fully engages with learners on the autism spectrum. It is here, even as we're still traveling along in our infancy as a school community, where I would argue that project-based learning schools, depending on how they are designed and nurtured, are *the* space for many students on the autism spectrum. PBL schools can potentially direct the enthusiasm of learners and provide them with a platform to enter into dialogue with adults and peers. Secondly, PBL schools afford all students authentic experiences outside the walls of a traditional environment. Through these experiences, learners on the autism spectrum are pushed to communicate in different ways and, as Temple Grandin suggests, "they learn self-agency" (Grandin, 2016, p. 40).

For this is the ultimate goal of all our learners – for them to become autonomous beings who can ask existential questions about their lives and push for meaningful answers and solutions that affect themselves and their communities. This is the power and potential of PBL. But first, we need to ground ourselves in what actually happens when a neurotypical brain learns and how this might be different in the brain of a person with autism.

How Does the Brain Learn?

Before fully exploring how project-based learning might provide an effective pathway for learning for those with autism spectrum disorders (ASDs), it's critical that we gain a foundational understanding of how the brain thinks and learns. As educators, if we're to create educative experiences and educative environments for all learners, including those on the autism spectrum, then it is imperative to peek inside both a neurotypical and non-neurotypical mind so that we can better serve all.

Those we might deem neurotypical are born with essentially the same brain, with approximately 100 billion neurons, or brain cells, which jump into action from Day 1. There are four principal sections, or lobes, of the brain, which are responsible for different tasks but ultimately work together. For example, as Janet Zadina suggests, "Reading can activate all lobes, but some specific regions are more activated than others" (2014, p. 11). The thalamus, which is essentially the control centre for directing signals to the various lobes, ensures that we're sensing, analyzing, thinking, and making connections in efficient ways – ways that are specific to each brain. The main part of the brain, the cerebrum, is covered by the cerebral cortex. The cerebral cortex receives information from the outside world, processes the inputs, and then executes a specific action or response, based on the processing of the signals. For example, if my son throws a baseball at my head, which he's apt to do, my eyes transmit that there's a ball coming toward my head, I sum up my options, and then I take appropriate action. This is the neurotypical way of processing information given to us by the outside world.

From a cellular perspective, we need neural connections, located throughout the brain, to send signals to other neurons and parts of the brain. Neuronal networks are indeed knowledge. As Zull (2002) asserts, "Not only is knowledge stored in the brain, it is produced by the brain through formation and change in neuronal networks" (p. 92). When we learn, we actually change physiologically! We can also deduce that what is critical for learning is the neuronal network that already exists in our learners. We know this from a theoretical perspective, as most educators have been shaped by the likes of Dewey and Kolb. We can articulate and envision a cycle of experience, one which begins at the core of what the learner already knows.

We're constantly signalling to our brains to create more neuronal networks or to scale back others. When we really learn, we tell our cells to thicken the myelin coating around the axon so that it can conduct electricity and knowledge faster. We make more complex connections in areas that are of interest, and we learn when we are calm and feeling good. Our neurotransmitters love it when we are engaged, relaxed, or full of joy. These are the emotions of learning that create powerful and complex neuronal networks.

But that's in a neurotypical brain.

The Brain with Autism

The brain with autism, on the other hand, doesn't work in the same way. Having said this, I acknowledge that autism is indeed on a spectrum, and so it manifests itself in many different ways. But there are two brilliant characterizations of the brain with autism that will serve us well. The first is by Barry Prizant, whose 2015 book *Uniquely Human: A Different Way of Seeing Autism*, changed how many engage with learners on the autism spectrum. Prizant, who comes with decades of experience working with learners and families, describes autism this way: "To be clear: Difficulty staying well-regulated emotionally and physiologically should be a core, defining feature of autism" (p. 18). Often, we describe and diagnose autism based on behaviours: X is acting this way; therefore, she must be on the autism spectrum. Prizant asks us to see autism as a way some people try to communicate – people whose brains often render them in a state of disequilibrium. He offers a description of the state of one person on the spectrum:

> The truth is that Ros finds the world overwhelming – a buzzing, confusing out-of-control reality filled with unexpected events and baffling social rules (p. 176).

The brain with autism senses the world differently than a neurotypical one. Signals from the thalamus might not be getting to the normal part of the brain and certain neuronal networks might not be pruned effectively. There is evidence suggesting that the brain with autism does not prune neuronal networks and therefore has too many synaptic connections. Signals are often crossed, misdirected, or overemphasized.

Temple Grandin describes the brain with autism in a similar manner:

> Autism is characterized by glitches in the brain's executive functioning. The 'departments' of the brain don't automatically communicate and come on-line

when presented with low or medium-interest tasks. And without this part of the brain clicking into gear, the ability to plan, organize and initiate goal-directed behaviour is impaired (p. 62).

Learners on the autism spectrum experience the world and universe differently than those with neurotypical brains. Some may see colours, hear words, or smell certain scents that send them into a panic. Many learners on the spectrum at our school are sensitive to noise, light, and the chaotic activity that seems to perpetually drive our projects and inquiry. It may seem like our project-based model would be antithetical to the brain with autism. But we found, as a faculty, that minor adjustments made our learning community a gradual place of success for our learners on the autism spectrum.

Why PBL?

Here are a few stories from the families and learners themselves that describe, better than I can, how project-based and student-centred environments can be effective, and also how they can be improved. These families are unbelievably supportive of their children and have made our learning community so much stronger. (The names of the learners have been changed. Learners and families have given their permission to participate in this chapter.)

Jason

Jason and his mom answered these questions together.

1. What is your story? What has been your journey with ASD?

    The journey through autism has been challenging to say the least. It started with Jason being just 12 months old sitting on the floor surrounded by marbles and not putting them in his mouth. I knew he was different then. By two years of age he still spoke a language he had invented himself and everyone around him thought it was cute. Little differences that set him apart. In elementary school – having a difficult time with noise made by his classmates, wanting to hang out with adults rather than his peers. Being "allergic" to his sister was one of the most difficult obstacles to get through to date. She couldn't come within a foot of him or touch any of his belongings without him spiralling out of control and being very violent toward her. Now he hugs his sister and tells her he loves her every day. Having Jason diagnosed and being able to understand him and the disorder was a relief in itself. We were able to move forward and support Jason with the entire family onboard.

2. What has been your experience with school before coming to the Maples Met?

In elementary school Jason felt he was labelled as "the autistic kid." Every day presented him with a new challenge. At a larger high school, he felt he started fresh but didn't like the way the school was set up. There was too much moving around; it was too big, with too many teachers. Maples Met felt liberating, as he says, because he was in the same class, with the same teacher, and he felt comfortable and was excited to work on the projects he wanted to do.

3. What successes have you encountered at the Met and why?

Thanks to Met's internship program, I was able to attend the Aviation Museum where I had a great working experience. At Met School, I learned how to do exhibitions, learned to be professional, and I got to follow my passions.

Steven

As answered by his mom:

1. What is your story? What has been your journey with ASD?

Steven was diagnosed as being on the spectrum while in kindergarten. It was hard to know what to expect with this diagnosis. We came to know that Steven is on the high-functioning end of the spectrum (Asperger's) and that while he is a very intelligent boy, his biggest challenges would be with social interactions and interpersonal relationships.

ASD often comes with other "bonus" diagnoses, and we found out as elementary school unfolded that he would also struggle with ADD (inattentive), anxiety issues, and tantrums. Steven's struggles were further compounded by the needs of his brother, who has ADHD, Tourette's,

Oppositional Defiant Disorder, and attributes of ASD as well. All of this culminated in a divorce, and Steven's dad left the province for over a year. The fallout of these changes left Steven with bouts of PTSD which complicated our attempts to manage his needs.

Steven spent grade 7 isolated at school for the most part. In grade 8, he was accepted into Montcalm School to help him deal with his anger and manage his behaviour through various individual therapies and support groups. He was transitioned back into mainstream classes with some modified subject material for grade 9. He found it difficult to adapt to the teaching methods of a typical classroom. Maples Met was suggested to us, and I'd heard wonderful things about the Met school model from moms whose teens are students at the Seven Oaks Met school.

Despite the wild ride these past few years, I've never been anything short of amazed by Steven's unique collection of abilities and idiosyncrasies. He has excelled in areas that I never imagined he would, such as self-expression and inward reflection. We have our day-to-day struggles, but he's come a long, long way.

2. What has been your experience with school before coming to the Maples Met?

During the elementary years, Steven had access to an educational assistant (EA), but there was a very low-functioning high-needs boy in his class who required one-on-one attention, and Steven sort of fell between the cracks. To deal with his behaviours (such as refusal to complete work, tantrums, and fleeing the classroom and sometimes the school), they tried many different strategies, none of which worked for very long before they flopped. Consequently, he was allowed to leave the class whenever he liked and did not accomplish much learning as a result. He was quite ill-prepared for grade 7.

The stresses of transferring to a new school, his friends distancing themselves from him, and his parents divorcing and fighting with his siblings all made things worse. Steven was finding it harder and harder to cope. He couldn't spend time in the class with the other kids and, again, his learning suffered.

While he was at a special school devoted to students on the spectrum, his mental and emotional wellness was their top priority. They made tremendous progress with Steven in those areas, but his schoolwork was all but ignored. He began grade 9 with barely a grade 5 education.

3. What successes have you encountered at the Met and why?

Putting Steven in Maples Met has been a complete change from any of his school experiences. Of course, it was an adjustment for him, but he is so happy to be there, and I cannot say that about any other program he's been involved in. He feels accepted by his peers and far better understood by the staff and students in general.

Steven has made great progress in his learning this year due to the dedication of his student advisor and principal. They've created an environment in which he feels comfortable. They've shown great patience and understanding in guiding him in the right direction, and they've supported him in making better choices and thinking critically about his options and what kind of student (and person) he wishes to be.

The feedback from his fellow students is invaluable to Steven. They're very encouraging of his efforts and they relate to him very well, helping him through the tough stuff. He hasn't felt that kind of support from classmates since the early years of elementary school. He's hungry to make friends, and while it's slow going, he's closer than he's ever been to making these important connections. This unique climate of understanding and acceptance starts at the top with the principal and trickles down to each staff member and student.

Anna
Response from Anna's parents:

1. What is your story? What has been your journey with ASD?

We learned Anna has ASD in 2017, so we are still wrapping our heads around what that means. We always could see signs of something, particularly around interpersonal relationships. We've had varied diagnoses of anxiety, OCD, ADHD, and now more recently Asperger's. Anna has taste and texture sensitivity, so her diet is limited, and her sense of smell is acute. She still struggles with depression and anxiety and ADHD. She has learned some cognitive coping skills to talk herself through some anxiety issues.

And she has a better understanding of who she is with the recent diagnosis of Asperger's.

2. What has been your experience with school before coming to the Maples Met?

There have always been struggles in school – frustrations, inappropriate actions, struggles to fit in and form friendships. Some peers within school were accepting and understanding of Anna, though it did not extend to friendships out of school, save for a couple of kids. She was picked on by some, and that leads her to assume her classmates will always be that way, so she is on the defensive. There were many phone calls from concerned teachers as we tried to figure out what we were dealing with and how to best help her. She struggled with math and her grades were average.

3. What successes have you encountered at the Met and why?

Anna has been able to apply her art skills to other areas of learning, which has greatly increased her interest and attendance at school. The small classroom size has benefited her, particularly in math, as the teacher was able to focus on her more. This was lost in her larger classrooms earlier.

Anna was able to explore Asperger's in her final exhibition, and though it made her anxious, she was able to present it in a way she felt comfortable with, and was able to disclose her own diagnosis to her classmates. It was received well, and enabled another student with Asperger's to talk about their own condition. The support from staff for her personal projects has been great.

She used to have anxiety when she was heading for school every morning. She does not have that with the Met school. Her thoughts and ideas are accepted, praised, and encouraged. Others are as excited about them as she is.

The Met has taught great interview skills. The teachers and principal are always available, and responses to emails or phone calls are always faster than we'd think. They are willing to work with us and support our child.

Anna's responses:

1. What is your story? What has been your journey with ASD?

I've recently been diagnosed with Asperger's, and ever since my diagnosis, I realize why I am the way I am.

2. What has been your experience with school before coming to the Maples Met?

    School was like riding a bike and the bicycle was in flames because it was hell.

3. What successes have you encountered at the Met and why?

    I have had successful exhibitions that mean a lot to me. My attendance at school is better because I can work through art and my ideas are accepted.

What Needs to Change?

It is clear that schools modelled around projects and inquiry, and that are student-centred, can be a positive and educative environment for students on the autism spectrum. In our case, when we finally got our act together (and we're still getting our act together) and began to adjust to the needs and talents of our learners, we witnessed tremendous growth, transformation, and learning.

But we've learned some valuable lessons in terms of how project-based learning needs to be designed in order for student success. Below are responses from our learners and families about how we need to change in order for learners on the spectrum to feel fully actualized.

Jason
Response from Jason:

1. What challenges have you faced at the Met and why?

    Even though I love the setup of Met School, it took a while to get used to. But I love it now. I love that I am in one area for my classes, that my principal is never too far away, and that I don't have a different teacher for every subject.

2. What are things the Met can do to better support students on the spectrum?

    People on the spectrum also have anxiety and are uncomfortable with unfamiliar surroundings – so maybe Met school can do more explaining around field trips, what's to be expected, what's going to be there, what's going to happen.

3. What do you wish people could know about autism?

   A lot of people with autism are able to have normal lives and I don't like how the media or a lot of people focus on the negative.

Reponse from Jason's mom:

4. What can the Met do to better support families?

   My son's Met School advisor has been absolutely supportive, understanding, extremely easy to talk to, and approachable. This has made the transition to this school a lot easier and the ongoing communication and a sense of family has been overwhelming. I know my son is in good hands when he's at school with people who want the best for him and are there supporting him and giving him all the opportunities that are available to other students

Steven

Response from Steven's mom:

1. What challenges have you faced at the Met and why?

   The only real challenge that comes to mind is the occasional need Steven has to be in a quiet place. Sometimes he needs his personal space to help with concentration and, at other times, he is overly anxious and needs to withdraw from the group. The layout of the school is such that there isn't really a dedicated quiet space for kids to have a self-imposed time-out. I can see the definite benefits of the comfortable group setting, which encourages collaboration, students assisting each other, sharing ideas more freely, etc. So, this is really a minor obstacle when measured against all the gains that are made in such an inclusive environment.

2. What are things the Met can do to better support students on the spectrum?

   In my own child, I've certainly noticed an increasing need to be heard and understood. I think a support group specifically for teens on the spectrum might be a safe environment for these kids to share the things that neurotypical students don't generally struggle with. Knowing they share the same challenges with other similar kids could make them feel much more connected to each other, and fare better in the group setting.

3. What can the Met do to better support families?

The Met already does an excellent job of seeing to each student's needs – not only as they pertain to their academic experience, but their Big Picture approach reaches each child as a whole entity, helping them make strides in every aspect of their lives. Steven brings his enthusiasm home and wants to do better with his chores, with his siblings, with the development of new hobbies and interests, and he's putting more and more thought into his own big picture – considering his career choices and taking better care of himself on the whole. This positive impact on our son has most definitely had a positive effect on our family, and we are grateful to Maples Met for their dedication and support.

Anna
Response from Anna's parents:

1. What challenges have you faced at the Met and why?

We face challenges in a few areas. She resists change in routine, resulting in homework meltdowns where she refuses to work, either at home or school. She is hyperfocused on her electronics and needs to be drawn back to task. She gets little work done at school unless reminded to focus. She could use an EA but does not qualify.

It is easy to forget – for Anna's teacher and for us – that though she is high-functioning, sometimes the expectations exceed her abilities. She has Asperger's. We have a list of characteristics that we occasionally review to put ourselves back on track.

The Met school offers some freedom based on work completed. Anna can't afford that freedom because of the lack of focus to complete work, so she feels "stupid" or "punished" when she sees others "rewarded." She wants to fit in, and does not like asking for help, because then she would stand out. She's not trying to be defiant or ornery – this is who she is.

Finding an internship for Anna is challenging. She's high-functioning, but needs assistance. She had been placed, but was left unsupervised when she needed it most. It was asked that she not continue. The rejection was a huge blow to her self-esteem. This happened pre-ASD diagnosis, and I don't think it would have been done that way had we known.

Interpersonal relationships continue to be a struggle.

2. What are things the Met can do to better support students on the spectrum?

Anna, like other kids on the spectrum, needs help socially with interpersonal relationships, boundaries, and forming friendships. Non-ASD students need help relating to the students with ASD in their midst. It does not happen easily or naturally, and it would be good if this were one of the supports given by the school. Anna has a desperate desire for friends. That desire, along with her other challenges, means she is vulnerable and needs guidance. Past experiences have made her defensive and judgmental, so there is stuff to overcome.

Internship help is needed until routines are established and understood by the student. This could involve pairing the student with another student, or ensuring mentors know that side-by-side instruction and modelling is required.

All kids on the spectrum should be welcome and included on exchanges and trips, and everything done to include them so they have the same positive experiences others have. I know it's hard to do, but it's not impossible.

Staff needs help understanding the spectrum too. Ball-catching and handwriting won't be strong. Anna is not strong on organization. She needs to be shown. And each child is different.

Treat our kids as kids first, then kids on the spectrum. They are not autistic, rather they are "kids with autism." They are not a diagnosis. They are fearfully and wonderfully made, intricate puzzles wrapped in mystery, and they are delights and gifts to us and the world. When Anna came to live with us, we felt we had won the lottery. We still feel that way.

3. What can the Met do to better support families?

We are learning. You bought the book *Aspergirls* by Rudy Simone (2010), and that has helped us.

Communication is big, and we need to know what goes well and what goes not so well before things become a bigger problem.

4. What do you wish people could know about autism?

Society is made up of differently abled people. Currently our school system does not deny any child an education. All are welcome regardless of their abilities. Those with troubled behaviours, visible disAbilities, and assessed mental disAbilities are offered and receive the services required in order to provide them with optimal learning opportunities. They receive counselling, psychological support, and one-on-one in-class support, to name a few. This enables these children to complete their education and move on in society with little to no continued outside support. In addition to an education, they have received the necessary guidance to enable them to function as a self-supporting member of society.

Within these classrooms there are a few children who do not exhibit any criteria that would allow them to receive required assessments and/or additional support. They do not have any behavioural concerns. They are not visibly disAbled. They appear to be "average," generally speaking. No red flags. No cause for alarm. These are the children in the classroom who suffer in silence. These are the children who struggle to learn in a traditional manner. These are the children who appear "normal," but have a mental disAbility.

These are the children who exhibit subtle clues. They may appear socially awkward, or have verbal but not written intelligence, etc. These children are usually on the lower end of the sliding scale, when finally assessed, hence the absence of clues. Their minds are so preoccupied that learning in a traditional setting is nearly impossible. Tests/exams are failed no matter how much they study. These children are smart, and their intelligence goes unnoticed. Or they appear so smart their disAbility goes unnoticed. They are pushed through the education system year after year. They do not qualify for an aide and rarely additional support, even after being assessed. They may be socially awkward, lonely, and struggle to fit into society. They may often be lost and left behind in "our" world.

These are the children who, as adults, end up unemployed and relying on social assistance or living on the street. Why? Because they were not given the opportunity of equal education and additional support throughout their youth.

Many, if not all, of these differently-abled Canadian citizens could be thriving members of our society. They are very capable people and most have a higher than average IQ. They *can* learn and are able to adapt to society as we know it. Instead, our current system allows them to slide on through and become "taxing" members of our community.

Without assessment and support, these children fight a bloodless war daily. They wake up every day and put on their armour and head out to face "our" world – a world in which everyone sees things differently than they do. A world of mass confusion. A lonely world where they fight alone.

The Rub

Learners on the autism spectrum each face different challenges and have unique skills and enthusiasm – hence, a spectrum. At our school, we've been able to slowly adapt to the needs and skills of our students, but the design of the school owes much to the successes experienced by our learners. Our design also poses some significant obstacles, which are not insurmountable, yet as we can glean from the incredible responses from our families, we have to do much better in some areas.

So, in answer to the initial question, why PBL? There is an overarching sense from Jason, Steven, and Anna that the simplicity of the school structure, its size, and the relationships they have with educators and mentors are key to their ability to feel engaged in this experiment we call school. For some learners on the autism spectrum, arriving at a project-based school immediately reduced a tremendous amount of anxiety and afforded an opportunity to engage in their passion. Often it is the anxiety that is the detriment to learning, as the wrong neurotransmitters are engaged. Dr. Barry Prizant speaks to the anxiety experienced by many learners on the autism spectrum, suggesting that when there is a lack of trust – trust in the system, trust in adults, or trust in their reactions – fear is triggered (p. 90). From our school's perspective, we notice this greatly when our students attend physical education at the larger high school. Many of our learners on the autism spectrum simply cannot handle the noise and chaos in a gym with one hundred other students. Prizant argues that "the opposite of anxiety isn't calm, it's trust" (p.73). Project-based learning, in the sense that it is student-centred, can be and arguably should be about building powerful relationships in an environment that is based on trust and where our learners are not overloaded.

Many learners on the spectrum suffer from anxiety and PTSD, and so an environment designed to limit this anxiety is what is required. (Bolic Balic et al., 2016) noted in a study on learners with Asperger's and ADHD that several factors determine learner success. These factors include small group sizes, individualized teaching methods, teachers who care, and emotional and practical support. PBL schools are designed for smaller sizes and one-on-one teaching and learning. This is the essence of PBL, if done well, and fully contingent on faculty who care deeply about the individual needs of their students, though we have struggled with attending to the practical support. I will get to this shortly.

Our learners also say that they love to follow their passions and enthusiasms. This is where PBL has really been of tremendous benefit for our learners. While many might see a deep passion or fixation, these enthusiasms, as articulated by Prizant, "can help children stay more engaged and attentive. They can be used to motivate learning and to enable participation in situations that might otherwise be difficult" (p. 60). These interests are where we can build trust and powerful relationships with learners and where we can begin to expand their understanding of the world – slowly and in a controlled way. We have seen tremendous success in project work at the Met, where Jason has created an incredibly deep sci-fi series that is seven books in the making. Steven has published his own book of fiction while at the same time curating an Apple computer museum, a passion of his. One student, who is a genius when it comes to animation and graphic design, created the graphic novel that is referred to at the end of this chapter, which explains her journey with Asperger's. All of these projects have provided the time and space to create meaningful relationships with our learners, allowing our faculty to understand how to give priority to the neuronal network of each learner while creating an environment of trust and reducing anxiety. As Prizant argues, "The best predictor of emotionally healthy children is having highly responsive caregivers" (p. 157).

Adapting to ASD

Where we need to change how we do things stems from the fact that a project-based school is often chaotic, unstructured, and overwhelming. Our experience as a learning community, and the feedback we have received from our learners, has really informed how we've designed project-based learning for all learners, not just those on the autism spectrum. The first task was to create an environment that was predictable. As Anna and her family suggested, the Met offers a tremendous amount of freedom, but this can be disastrous for many learners. What we've had to do is really carve out what each day will look like for our learners. As our learners are always seeking to self-regulate, they need an environment that is predictable and one they can navigate. This navigation comes in the form of daily routines, written lists, chunking, rewards for task completion, and daily one-on-one meetings to ensure that everyone is clear on what needs to be achieved for that day. We've also found that some of our learners need to arrive and leave at different times, and require times when they can go for walks and when they can chill out.

The latter point of chilling out is another area where we struggled as a project-based school. By its nature, our project-based school can become pretty loud, full of energy, and overwhelming for some. In our first few years, we were a school within a school and our space was limited. We didn't find a way to create a space where learners could go to decompress and relax. In recent months, we've created a safe space for learners to go to when they feel overwhelmed and when the world is overloading their senses – a space in which they can feel safe.

Many of our learners on the autism spectrum also feel that creating meaningful relationships with peers is incredibly difficult. This is certainly a theme in the responses from our learners and a significant challenge for them. Social awkwardness has also presented some challenges related to our internship program, through which learners engage with mentors in the field to pursue meaningful projects. As Bolic Baric suggests about the school experience for many on the autism spectrum:

> School was permeated with difficulties in social relationships with peers and difficult emotional experiences, including anxiety and depressed mood. These influenced emotional well-being in school and were found to influence the participants' learning ability. The analysis demonstrated that social interaction with peers was characterized by misunderstanding and a sense of being excluded, ignored, and rejected by peers, often with prolonged bullying (p. 187).

At the Met, our learners often struggle with cultivating relationships with peers and often feel excluded. While our faculty have purposely created experiences whereby all our learners venture out in the field, travelling to various cities in Canada and camping in the Manitoba wilderness, it's still very difficult for learners on the autism spectrum to connect with other learners and

Some pages from a graphic novel created by a Maples MET student on the autism spectrum, presented on the next three pages with permission. The entire novel can be viewed at https://tinyurl.com/y8djvk9

create friendships. Firstly, in response to this, we've worked hard to connect our learners on the autism spectrum with mentors in the community who completely understand where our learners are coming from. Secondly, we've created a Tuesday morning program where all learners, not just learners on the autism spectrum, are invited to come learn basic cooking skills while at the same time learning how to connect with other learners. While this program is in its infancy, our initial observations are that it is critical for learners to be pushed and to learn how to communicate in public. Temple Grandin speaks of this push by her mother as a child, and is a strong advocate for getting learners out there, out of their bedrooms, and into the "real world."

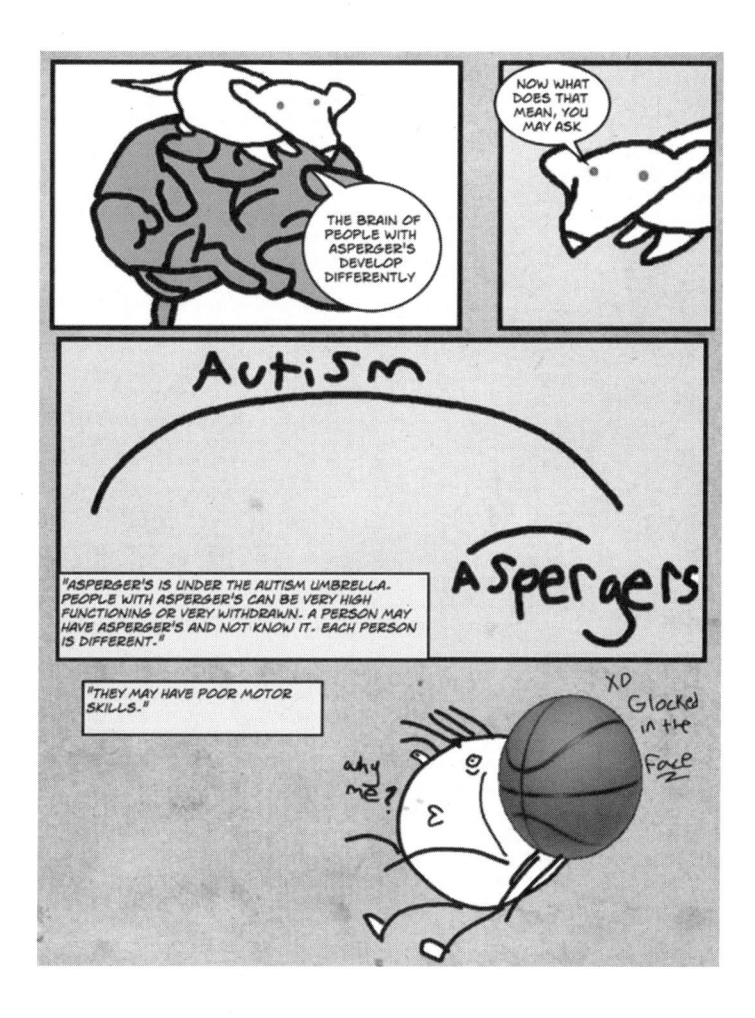

While most of what we've learned as a learning community seems like common sense and simply good pedagogical practice, we're still challenged each day to meet the needs and talents of all our learners. We know, however, that real projects, those that stretch the minds of our learners and ask them to consider major questions about our universe, are powerful motivators for learning. For our students on the autism spectrum, projects are a way in – a way for our faculty to engage with the neuronal networks and their connecting hearts, and a starting point for our learners to connect with us and with learning. What is paramount is that our project-based environments need to take into account many challenges that exist for brains with autism. For project-based learning schools to be a place for relationships and powerful learning for learners on the autism spectrum, they need to have the following:

- Faculty and staff who care and are devoted to learners and to research.
- A structured and predictable day for each learner.
- A sensory-specific environment for each learner.
- A unique and personalized learning plan for each learner.
- Programming that teaches life skills as well as social skills.
- Mentors in the community who understand autism spectrum disorders.
- High expectations for academic success coupled with high levels of support.

- Open communication with families.
- Access to community supports.

References

Bolic Baric, V., Hellberg, K., Hemingson, H., & Kjellberg, A. (2016). Support for learning goes beyond academic support: Voices of students with Asperger's disorder and attention deficit hyperactivity disorder. *Autism, 20*(2), 183-195.

Grandin, T., & Moore, D. (2015). *The loving push: How parents and professionals can help spectrum kids become successful adults.* Arlington, TX: Future Horizons.

Prizant, B.M. (2015). *Uniquely human: A different way of seeing autism.* New York, NY: Simon & Schuster.

Simone, R. (2010). *Aspergirls: Empowering females with Asperger syndrome.* London, England: Jessica Kingsley Publishers.

Tang, G., Gudsnuk, K., Kuo, S.H., Cotrina, M.L., Rosoklija, G., Sosunov, A., … Sulzer, D. (2014, September 3). Loss of mTOR-dependent macroautophagy causes autistic-like synaptic pruning deficits. *Neuron, 83*(5), 1131-1143. Retrieved from http://go.galegroup.com.uml.idm.oclc.org/ps/i.do? p=HRCA&sw=w&u=univmanitoba&v=2.1&it=r&id= GALE%7CA383279149&asid=24d409183812226e85586a3f43baaf6f

Zadina, J. (2014). *Multiple pathways to the student brain: Energizing and enhancing instruction.* San Francisco, CA: Jossey-Bass.

Zull, J. (2002). *The art of changing the brain: Enriching the practice of teaching by exploring the biology of learning.* Sterling, VA: Stylus.

About the Author
Sid has been teaching for 24 years with the Winnipeg School Division. Her classroom experiences range from multi-age grades 1 to 6 to working as an inquiry support teacher. She loves spending time with her three adult daughters and her friends. She loves working out and, most of all, loves to learn new things!

Who Should Read This Chapter?
Teachers and administrators.

The Theme of This Chapter in Two Words
Overcoming roadblocks.

As an Educator, What Are You Passionate About?
Watching students take ownership of their learning.

CHAPTER 8

Getting People on Board the Project-Based Learning Bus

Sid Williamson, King Edward Community School
Winnipeg, Manitoba, Canada

I am a support teacher in an inner-city school, with a population of approximately 330 students from nursery to grade 6. One of the roles that I fulfill is that of inquiry support teacher. This involves working with teachers on methods for using inquiry as a foundation for learning in their classrooms. I support and mentor teachers as they move from teacher as leader to teacher as facilitator and collaborator. Through inquiry and project-based learning, learning communities can become dynamic learning environments where students are motivated and excited about the learning. This journey can be intimidating for teachers who have never observed or worked with those whose classrooms support this pedagogy. Barriers are present from beyond the classroom and from within as we move toward enabling that gradual release of responsibility and building capacity so that students can become independent learners.

My experience in teaching a three-grade, multi-aged, child-centred classroom for 14 years has provided me with a firsthand understanding of the strength of inquiry-based learning. My primary role was to support my students as they learned how to find answers for themselves, to teach them where to go to find answers, to encourage their big questions, and to provide materials and directions on how to use them to find information. A big focus was on collaborative learning. Much of the time, students worked with partners or groups. Some worked independently. Some moved in and out of groups as needed. This ability to work flexibly supported students who needed think time on their own, and also encouraged and developed skills they needed to work in a group. My role was as facilitator. Because much of my work – organizing, planning, identifying skills, and finding materials – began early on, I was able to support my students more effectively through the course of their inquiry. I had more one-on-one or small-group time and was able to have many conversations around where they were at and where they needed to go. Out of a read-aloud exercise (*Hana's Suitcase* by Karen Levine, for example) came classroom conversations about what they might do if they found an empty suitcase. What would their stories be? How would they fill their suitcases, and who would their stories represent? This became a year-long journey into their own family stories, with each student creating histories and understandings and representing them in "suitcases" that told the stories of their families and cultural backgrounds. These stories mapped journeys of individuals from their histories and the contributions they had made to the rest of the world. It was a powerful journey for all of us (parents included) that came out of the students' curiosity and questions. This is the power of PBL that I have tried to share with the teachers I support.

In my third year as an inquiry support teacher, I've come to understand the barriers that face many teachers before they implement PBL. With little or no exposure to classrooms that function from an inquiry perspective, it's difficult to see how it can work. Teachers often have little or no time to visit other classrooms to see others at work. Teaching is, by its very nature, an isolating profession. It is difficult to see ourselves and to effect change when we don't really know what it is we're trying to change. In my role, I've learned to engage slowly with teachers. I've also realized that my role cannot be imposed on them. Shifting pedagogy is a journey that must begin with trust and the understanding that it takes time to change our practice. Providing opportunities to visit PBL classrooms is a great way to begin the journey. This allows time to observe, think, and develop relationships and conversation that can continue over time.

Another barrier is the fact that teachers are overloaded. There is so much that we're responsible for, so many roles we need to fill. In the elementary stream, we teach English language arts, maths, science, social sciences, health, art, and almost anything else one can think of. We're social workers and nurses, and we act *in loco parentis*. We are problem solvers. We book field trips, locate lunches, find clothing, and connect with social services, daycares, and family members. We are learners who try to keep on top of changes and new understandings in how children learn. We run clubs at lunch and after school. We meet and share with colleagues. We are innovators and users of technology. Our day does not end at 3:30 PM. We mark, prepare, and lose sleep over our students. It is an extremely demanding career. For some teachers, shifting pedagogy is just one more thing on their plates – one more thing on top of so many others.

The demands of assessment and data collection support a more traditional classroom. Data collection has become a large part of teaching. Assessment is ongoing and is based on designing experiences and then assessing if learning occurred during this experience. Programmed assessment takes a great deal of time. Inputting data online is required, which also takes time, time that is taken after the school day. Report-card comments are based largely on these tools. School results are collated and shared with staff and with other schools.

Public perception plays a role here as well. Attention is paid to how poorly Manitoba students do in reading, math, and science when compared to students across Canada. School divisions often respond to this kind of press with a knee-jerk reaction. They look for a quick fix, looking to a program to solve the problem rather than looking at what *is* working and where and how those best practices can be applied in ways that support student success. Trying to find consistency in programming seems to be the overriding perspective of many school divisions – that if all students are doing the same programs, we will get a better picture of where problems may be and how we can address those problems. I've often heard the comment that many teachers are not doing a good enough job of teaching reading and math, and that by forcing them to all teach a "good" program – a program that has some research to back it up – teachers will then improve their practice. And yet a one-size-fits-all approach to teaching and assessment has proven to be more detrimental than beneficial; that standardized approach does not work for many learners and certainly does not support students as they move into a world that is constantly changing.

A more ambitious, longitudinal comparative study by Jo Boaler and colleagues in England in 1997 and 1998 followed students over three years in two schools that were similar in student achievement and income levels. One school, a traditional one, featured teacher-directed whole-class instruction organized around texts, workbooks, and frequent tests in tracked classrooms. Instruction in the other school used open-ended projects in heterogeneous classrooms.

The study found that although students had comparable learning gains on basic mathematics procedures, significantly more project-learning students passed the national exam in year three than those in the traditional school. Although students in the traditional school "thought that mathematical success rested on being able to remember and use rules," according to the study, the project-learning students developed more flexible and useful mathematical knowledge.

The rise in interest in the Makerspace movement appears to be increasing interest in PBL. There is more understanding that traditional classrooms have less student engagement. More students are bored and stressed out, and are not empowered to "own" their learning. The Makerspace movement is drawing a great deal of attention to the fact that when students feel empowered and interested in what they're learning, engagement improves. Teachers who are feeling the pinch of time limitations can implement maker programs slowly and incrementally. Teachers can incorporate "passion projects" or "choice time" at any grade level and in small time slots, allowing themselves the opportunity to develop their own understandings and comfort with and of PBL. As John Spencer and A.J. Juliani say, "Choice drives student ownership of their learning. This kicks empowerment into high gear, and ultimately leads to learning that is intrinsic, powerful and deep" (2017).

We're also preparing students for the new realities of the work world. Employers are looking for individuals who are critical thinkers, creative, and collaborative. These are the basic tenets of PBL. A standardized approach to learning is not going to support 21st century demands on our students and certainly does not allow for creating a PBL classroom.

Project-based learning can become one more thing to do rather than a different way of teaching. Again, I would suggest that the most effective ways to encourage and see change include having opportunities to visit classrooms, be mentored and supported, and given time to shift pedagogy. Ultimately, PBL and inquiry provide more time to work with students and less time planning for five or six different content areas. Once it's established, teachers spend less time on the minutiae of planning and more time supporting students throughout their learning journey.

References

Barron, B. (2008). Powerful learning: Studies show deep understanding derives from collaborative methods. *Edutopia*. Retrieved from https://www.edutopia.org/inquiry-project-learning-research

Boaler, J. (1999). Participation, knowledge, and beliefs: A community perspective on mathematics learning. *Educational Studies in Mathematics, 40*(3), 259-281.

Levine, K. (2002). *Hana's Suitcase*. Toronto, ON: Second Story Press.

Spencer, J., & Juliani, A.J. (2017). *Empower: What happens when student own their learning*. IMPress, LP.

About the Authors

Dr. Eva Brown is a passionate teacher educator at Red River College in Winnipeg and the University of Calgary. She has over thirty years of teaching experience in various disciplines at the junior and senior high school level, and in higher education. Her focus is seeking leading and learning opportunities for her students and herself that will have an impact on education. Eva demonstrates her strong belief that educators must model their learning to their students. Her research interests include designing learning for technology-rich collaborative learning environments and the development of research skills in new teachers so that they can become teachers as researchers.

Theresa Armstrong completed her Bachelor of Education degree in the spring of 2018 from Red River College and the University of Winnipeg. Her teaching focus is business, technology, and mathematics. Before entering education, Theresa earned her accounting designation and has worked for over fifteen years in private and nonprofit organizations. Theresa turned to education, after two years of teaching postsecondary business courses, to learn the essential pedagogy necessary to be an effective teacher. Theresa's passion for teaching comes from a desire for all her students to succeed in 21st-century competencies.

Who Should Read This Chapter?

Teacher educators, pre-service teachers, education policy makers, teachers, administrators.

The Theme of This Chapter in Five Words

Experiencing PBL in teacher education.

As Educators, What Are You Passionate About?

Best opportunities for learning to prepare students for the changing world.

CHAPTER 9

Experiencing Project-Based Learning: Beginning in Teacher Education

Theresa Armstrong, a teacher candidate in the Teacher
Education Program at Red River College, and Dr. Eva Brown,
one of Theresa's instructors in the RRC program
Winnipeg, Manitoba, Canada

In a globally competitive world enabled by technology, it is important that people have the skills to communicate and collaborate, to solve problems and think critically, and to develop new ideas and create knowledge. It therefore seems logical that students learn these skills to become successful citizens who are able to contribute to humanity in a meaningful way. How are these skills being taught? Do our teachers know how to model these skills for their students? Perhaps the most important question is whether or not our new teachers are learning to design project-based lessons to provide their students with the skills that the world demands.

Industrial-age society required schools to give knowledge to learners using a systematic approach so that everyone knew the same things and performed in the same manner in order for assembly lines to be successful. The knowledge-based economy does not require the same education format as that of an industrial age. Schools that adhere to a traditional teacher-centred format are not providing their students with the opportunities needed to become globally competitive citizens for today and for the future. Education needs to change from using teacher-centred approaches to that of student-centred approaches, or an inquiry-based pedagogy, to meet the needs – and demands – of the world. Reformation in education is a slow process because much change needs to occur to bring industrial-age schools into knowledge-based learning environments.

All stakeholders must be involved in this reformation, including policy makers, teacher education programs, teacher educators, administrators, teachers, students, and parents. "Traditional educational practices no longer provide prospective teachers with all the necessary skills for teaching students to survive economically in today's workplace" (UNESCO, 2008, p. 1).

There is plenty of research (Clifford, Friesen, & Lock, 2004; Dede, 2010; Thomas & Brown, 2011) to support the need for reformation in education that implements inquiry-based pedagogy and project-based learning. Manitoba Education (2016) has developed the Literacy with ICT K-12 Continuum. This continuum is based on seven embedded supporting principles:

- inquiry
- constructivist learning
- higher-level critical and creative thinking
- reaching deeper understanding
- gradual release of responsibility
- digital citizenship
- multiple literacies for the 21st century

Inquiry is described by the Galileo Network (2004) as follows:

> Inquiry is a dynamic process of being open to wonder and puzzlement and coming to know and understand the world. As such, it is a stance that pervades all aspects of life and is essential to the way in which knowledge is created. Inquiry is based on the belief that understanding is constructed in the process of people working and conversing together as they pose and solve the problems, make discoveries and rigorously testing the discoveries that arise in the course of shared activity" (http://galileo.org/teachers/designing-learning/articles/what-is-inquiry/).

It is important that teacher candidates learn from teacher educators who model these student-centred approaches. It is essential that teacher educators model inquiry-based pedagogy in their lessons so that teacher candidates have the opportunity to experience student-centred approaches. New teachers often need professional development from the first day of their teaching career to learn to become pedagogically and technologically fluent (Plair, 2007) because they have not been provided with opportunities that prepared them to design lessons that infused technology for teaching and learning.

Why are our students not allowed to experience project-based learning? Is it because we don't know what it is? Is it because we're unfamiliar with the benefits? Is it because we're unsure of content knowledge? Is it because we don't have the skills or self-efficacy to facilitate it? Is it because our hands are tied with standardized testing? Is it because we're discouraged by our administrators? In a recent study that explored the design of technology-enabled learning experiences in teacher education and how they translate into classroom practice, Brown (2017) noted that we teach the way we were taught. This fact makes it important for teacher educators to model teaching practices that pre-service teachers need to develop as effective teachers in the 21st century. If teacher educators lack the pedagogical knowledge to prepare pre-service teachers, then "without a discrete and identifiable knowledge (base)-for-practice, those who teach teachers can only teach as they were taught" (Goodwin et al., 2014, p. 13). Brown (2017) also noted that "teacher educators who teach the way they were taught may be modelling twenty-year-old or older practices and norms, which is simply not good enough for contemporary classrooms" (p. 21). The findings of Goodwin et al. (2014) speak to the concern that teacher educators are not modelling appropriate practices for pre-service teachers because they themselves lack this skill. As a result, "they cannot be expected to design quality teacher preparation programs, envision innovation, and conduct meaningful research in teacher education" (p. 16).

Red River College Teacher Education provides students with inquiry-based pedagogy instruction and practice. Teacher candidates study various student-centred approaches and have the opportunity to practise these approaches in their microteaching lessons in authentic classrooms – with real students. Theresa was one of these pre-service teachers in RRC's teacher education program. She shares her experiences in the next part of this chapter.

Illustrations and Perspectives from a Pre-Service Teacher

Inquiry and problem-based learning was a new and exciting concept for me. This was not what was modelled to me throughout my public education experience, with teacher-centred lectures and classroom time to solve problems or write essays being the order of the day. The focus was on practice, rote memorization, and the *do as I say* model, with little room for creativity, individual interest, or collaboration.

During my education at Red River College, I've been introduced to student-centred approaches through courses and then have been expected to model this approach through my practicum placements. Therefore, the practice is not reimagining the process, but is the carry-through of what has been taught. I found the small, intimate classes at Red River College important in learning new approaches for gaining insight and feedback from authentic learning opportunities. What follows are some of the reflections of my learning journey.

Curriculum is important! Nobody would deny this statement. It has a proven track record of academic and practical importance to students and has been reviewed by educational and industry experts alike. At the start of my teacher-education program, my first impression was that inquiry was a new approach that tossed curriculum to the side and focused on student-initiated topics of interest. This is simply not the case. Curriculum is still the underlying foundation of what students learn through inquiry, and teachers need to facilitate curriculum objectives in student projects or research. It is how the students learn academic outcomes that changes with inquiry; thus, the process of learning is the focus, not the product.

One of my primary concerns, especially after hearing so much about student-centred approaches from other teachers, is time. How would one facilitate such a process when time is limited and outcomes are numerous? My discovery is that education has placed much emphasis on quantity in terms of learning outcomes and little to none on quality. Is the goal for the student to do well on ten different topics found in a standardized test, or for them to be able to apply and explain eight topics in their own words? At an ASCD (2017) conference during my teacher-education program, Dr. Yong Zhao, the keynote speaker, explained that the concept of academic excellence is important, but so is globalmindedness, creativity, and enhancing individual talents. Are these of equal importance? I will explore this a little later. Adding inquiry into teaching can help promote the additional objectives that Dr. Zhao and so many others speak about. It can function as active, creative learning (quality) while enforcing learned objectives (quantity).

Facilitation is a skill. Speaking as a pre-service teacher, there were times when I felt overwhelmed with all the required skills I needed to master when conducting a lesson: the ability to consider long-term planning, assessment strategies, universal design for learning (UDL), sustainability ... and the list goes on.

Learning what inquiry actually is and how to facilitate it within a classroom is another skill that needs to be nurtured and practised. I've learned that there is no right way to accomplish this task, which is influenced by a variety of factors. First and foremost, inquiry is about your own personal journey to embracing inquiry – by defining it, acknowledging the benefits, and practising it. I've found in my limited experience that inquiry has the potential to provide cross-curricular links, foster student engagement, and promote the committing of learning to long-term memory.

Obviously, teachers need to be introduced to the topic, and preferably to experience it throughout K-12 education, but they also need to understand its importance in postsecondary education. It was here that it was introduced to me. In one of my classes, we were given an inquiry project where we learned about something that we wanted to learn more about. The inquiry project was to detail the process of learning about our topic. Process over product was key. I found initial research was helpful, along with asking questions from a trusted source; however, I did not ask an *expert* until later in the process. Practice and feedback were also important steps along the way.

A course in our teacher education program on course development incorporated an inquiry project for the whole term. We learned what makes up a course and applied it to a course we developed on our own. In order to become proficient, we needed to practise a skill and make mistakes along the way. As with every other skill, feedback is very important in order to help you refine your process. It can feel like a long and painful journey at times, but if pre-service teachers keep the end results of student engagement and learning in mind, the process may be more tolerable. Although this may be a subjective skill, and hard to assess for the purposes of an interview, every education student needs to learn a variety of approaches.

Parents and administrators expect exceptional and engaging education for all students, and teachers need to be able to design lessons to the best of their ability to meet this expectation. Obviously, everyone shares responsibility for this outcome, but you are only in charge of yourself, and the onus on pre-service teachers is to practise, take feedback from mentors, and keep learning. It's analogous to a baby starting to walk: a baby needs to see others do it, see the benefits, practise, and then experience the stumbles along the way. I have stumbled in my own journey of delivering inquiry lessons and projects, but I give myself permission to explore and make mistakes.

Another factor that can influence your approach is school culture. Although it can provide challenges, my experience has been that it will not prevent you from using inquiry approaches. Depending on previous experiences, some students, parents, and administrators may not be familiar with such approaches. There is no single answer that is right for all courses, schools, grades, or times. I'd initially thought that inquiry involved big projects that students would complete over the course of a semester., but inquiry can be delivered in short, five-minute segments during a teacher-centred lesson. It may not be the focal point of the lesson, but it can provide short bursts of variety and engagement.

In a lesson delivered to a grade 11 class, I incorporated a short inquiry portion. However, although the topic and questions were planned out, my timing was off. Teachers need to pay attention to student reactions and responses to determine the right amount of time for them to research an answer. It can be difficult to allow students the time to research answers when you're already an expert. Exit slips and formative assessment can help you determine what, if anything, you can do differently.

I've also made the mistake of turning a student-centred lesson into a teacher-centred lesson. I have a passion for certain areas of study and want students to learn and enjoy that area as well. I found that, although I may have practised the lesson multiple times, it's important for me to keep in mind that students are hearing about this content for the first time and don't have the same experience that I have. They are also are at a different developmental level in their lives. It is key to relax and be flexible within inquiry and lessons in general.

With so many concepts and approaches to learn, I've found it best to focus on what is most important when completing practicum placements and preparing for the future. The first step is to determine how many units you need to accomplish, how many lessons per unit you'll have, and what assessment strategies you'll use. Instructions for assessment need to be clear and expressed both verbally and in written form. Question time should also be provided so that students can ask for clarification.

It is when tackling the individual lesson plans that you can consider student-centred approaches. Without the foundation of long-term planning and communication of assessment, even the best intentions for student-centred approaches fall short, as time and grades become barriers to the process. I've found practicum placements extremely helpful as communication with your mentor can help speed the process and identify potential pitfalls. Taking on a significant course load can be a daunting task and many pre-service teachers are tired from meeting the demands placed on a full-time teacher.

Although mistakes are expected, it's been important for me to experience success in practicum placements and student-centred approaches because it propels me to keep initiating such projects. Success can take multiple forms, as when I experience a quiet class because everyone is busy working away, or when students ask me outside of class time about the project.

One inquiry project that went really well involved my co-designing an accounting project with another teacher from a different school. She helped provide the assessment and curriculum pieces and I prepared the questions for further thought. The students from both classrooms were mixed together in groups and everyone had a task to complete for marks. Each group used a Google spreadsheet and Google document to make sharing easier. It allowed students to gain multiple perspectives on the topic and to see the application of taxes in real life.

I've found that when students are going to present their project or have their ideas and thoughts posted for the class to see, they're initially awkward but soon give more time and attention to what they write or present. It is with this in mind that I've started to preplan a student-centred project for my next practicum placement.

The following blog posts, written by Theresa, reflect on teaching and learning.

My Path to Teaching

My journey began three years ago with a passion for teaching, a drive to share my knowledge, and the challenge or desire to be an effective teacher for a wide range of students. This takes considerable effort, thought, and patience. It involves a reciprocal relationship with your students where they learn from you and you learn from them.

For the most part I enjoyed my education growing up, which involved teacher-centred pedagogies with individual assignments and standardized tests for which a good memory was a definite asset. However, so many of our students don't learn effectively in this type of environment. We have students who don't test well, those who are visual and kinesthetic learners, and those who need to see the end purpose in their learning to make progress. These students in our classes need to be nurtured just as much as others. Our focus cannot be on the best grade outcomes, but on learning for all students regardless of their level or ability. There needs to be a shift in the paradigm from how many students reach the top rung of the ladder to how many students move along the rungs. Education is a journey and not an end result.

Manitoba Education has a mandate to provide all students with rich and meaningful learning opportunities. As teachers we need to strive to educate ourselves about such opportunities. Inquiry is a great student-centred pedagogy that fosters real-world application with a cross-curricular approach. This pedagogy increases student engagement because there is a degree of student choice within the learning, including a choice in how the information is obtained, and the cross-curricular approach helps students to make connections between different kinds of information.

Do you support inquiry-based pedagogy? What drives your passion as an educator? If you're looking for resources, I've found the Galileo network (http://galileo.org/) a helpful resource.

Flexible 21st-Century Learning

For this blog post I decided to comment on cross-curricular instruction and flexible seating arrangements. Education hasn't changed very much in 60 or 70 years; however, we're on the edge of some new and exciting trends within education. As a new teacher, I can't wait to employ some of these strategies.

The first topic I researched was cross-curricular instruction. In an article by Force, Kotch, Hendon, and Rivera (2016) about equipping teachers for such instruction, the authors indicate that students need repetition and practical approaches to connect subject material. Force et al. (2016) believe that students' experiences with technology through cross-curricular activities will result in long-term retention of skills and concepts. Obviously, there is overlap between topics, so why not embrace it? We've come from a background of one-room schoolhouses; with population growth we were able to employ more specialized teachers and curriculum became separated. However, this trend doesn't mean we can't tie trends, technology, and topics together. Cross-curricular instruction allows students to connect information and formulate solid knowledge through repetition and application.

The second topic I researched was flexible seating arrangements. As I read the article by Douglas (2017), "Ditching the Desks," a question came up for me: How many secondary students do you know who say that school is boring? The number is quite high. If we just isolate seating arrangements, perhaps we can find part of the reason. Have you tried to sit in a chair all day, not talk, and be on task, especially with a subject that doesn't interest you? You might find it hard to do. Flexible seating and classrooms designed by both teacher and students can be beneficial for all. Such seating arrangements promote comfort, and if we're comfortable, we're ready to learn. This could mean students in pods or groups, in reading chairs, or at counter-height tables that allow for taller chairs or let students stand. We need to think how we're comfortable when learning. Active learning with cross-curricular instruction requires a variety of flexible seating arrangements.

Although these topics are not stated directly as part of the vision of education in Manitoba, Canada, or elsewhere, in my opinion they're pathways for some of the stated objectives. Creative and critical thinking is part of the mandate of Manitoba Education and elsewhere. How can students create when they're not comfortable? How can we ask our students to think critically unless they connect with the subject material? With these questions in mind, perhaps more of our discussion will touch upon these topics.

Success in the 21st Century

Being successful in educating students requires us as educators to be aware of 21st century learning skills. These skills cannot be undermined in the face of the enormous pressure to achieve high academic excellence in standardized test scores. Yes, policy makers need to change assessment practices and have a collaborative focus (both locally and globally) and incorporate technology and inquiry-based projects that involve creative and critical thinking skills. However, as educators we can't wait until policy catches up with what the workforce is demanding from our students. *ISTE Standards* (2016) and the

New Horizon Report (2016) are international documents that teachers can follow to help guide their students. Teachers need to showcase their students' work and align curriculum standards with deeper learning opportunities.

A study by Whitty and Clarke (2012) found that approximately one-third of teachers in Ireland use ICT, or games, to help students learn concepts. Technology is growing rapidly and to deny its existence is to turn a blind eye to the changing dynamics of a globally competitive world. Technology needs to be infused into the K-12 curriculum in Manitoba, but we do not always see this happening in practice. Are teachers trained in this area? Is there enough technology available for the students? Do teachers feel other pressures that prevent them from using technology? Why can't learning be fun? What are we afraid of?

Whitty and Clarke suggest that Irish mathematics teachers are in a similar struggle to Manitoba teachers. There are many needs within a large classroom. Educators want the best learning for their students, so many incorporate various technology methods to ensure globally competitive learning opportunities. This means we need to find cross-curricular, inquiry-based, collaborative projects that involve technology to reach curriculum outcomes. Students will benefit from understanding how things intertwine, will be more engaged, will generally enjoy what they did, and will practise or take the learning outside of the classroom. These are the building blocks for critical thinking that will allow our students to solve the problems of tomorrow that are unknown today. These problems will require a team approach from a group of diverse thinkers.

Conclusion

The education system isn't broken. It was designed for an industrial age that has passed and isn't adequate to meet the needs of the 21st century. The world now emphasizes a knowledge-building economy. Reynolds (2014), in a book entitled *Imagine It Better*, illustrates visions from educators of what an effective education system could and should look like to provide this generation and beyond with skills for their future. The ideas shared by the experienced and passionate educators in this book provide the hope that school can and will be useful and even fun, a place where students and teachers learn together and construct knowledge – a place where students want to go.

School cannot be a test of memory any longer, but a place of understanding where creativity and innovation are encouraged. "Begin properly with the child and we will need no competition between countries any more" (Hargreaves, 2014, p. 13). Innovation is messy, and we'd best get used to it if we're going to provide our students with the education they need to become globally competitive. The teacher's role has changed. "Warrior teaching requires risk-taking, playfulness, and imagination" (Grande, 2014, p. 18).

The teaching profession needs to become one where teachers want to teach, have a passion for teaching, and are respected and given the autonomy needed to make decisions for the best student learning. Teachers need to aspire to ontological knowing and become researchers. This approach requires a paradigm shift. Developing an education system that is effective for the 21st century begins in teacher preparation with programs that are rigorous, reflective, and active. Teacher education needs to be reformed and there needs to be a new system of teacher promotion and professional development. Teachers need to be "inspired and committed to keep growing and learning – forever!" (Darling-Hammond, 2014, p. 160). That is what will bring back the *professional* into the teaching profession. Society must promote and support a learning culture for reformation to take place.

Teacher education needs to be at the forefront, producing new teachers who are equipped to translate their campus learning into their classroom practice. Many new teachers are not provided opportunities to design learning using inquiry approaches with technologies – in meaningful ways that develop critical thinking and problem-solving skills – and they're not prepared to make changes. These new teachers enter their classrooms teaching in old ways because of the way they were taught. Many new teachers need professional development from day one of their careers to be effective teachers in the 21st century.

The world has changed and continues to change – rapidly. Teaching in the 21st century is indeed exciting! It's a tough job and not for the faint of passion. Teaching begins with passion, and requires effort and work and time. It's time for action, beginning in teacher education. One step at a time, we need to do something to create change. Together we can do it!

References

Brown, E. (2017). *Exploring the design of technology enabled learning experiences in teacher education that translate into classroom practice* (Doctoral dissertation). Retrieved from ProQuest Dissertations and Theses database.

Clifford, P., Friesen, S., & Lock, J. (2004). *Coming to teaching in the 21st century: A research study conducted by the Galileo Educational Network*. Calgary, AB: The Galileo Educational Network, University of Calgary.

Darling-Hammond, Linda. (2014). Learning to teach in the twenty-first century. In L. Reynolds (Ed.), *Imagine it better: Visions of what school might be* (150-160). Portsmouth, NH: Heinemann.

Dede, C. (2010). Comparing frameworks for 21st century skills. In J. Bellance & R. Brandt (Eds.), *21st century skills: Rethinking how students learn* (51-75). Bloomington, IN: Solution Tree Press.

Douglas, T. (2017). Ditching the desks: Flexible learning spaces focus on helping students be productive, comfortable. *Entrsekt, 3*(3), 30-38.

Force, C., Kotch, M., Hendon, M., & Rivera, K. (2016). Equipping teachers for cross-curricular instruction. *Business Education Forum, 71*(2), 18-20.

Goodwin, A. L., Smith, L., Souto-Manning, M., Cheruvu, R., Tan, M. Y., Reed, R., & Taveras, L. (2014). What should teacher educators know and be able to do? Perspectives from practicing teacher educators. *Journal of Teacher Education, 65*(4), 284+. Retrieved from http://go.galegroup.com.ezproxy.lib.ucalgary.ca/ps/i.do?id=GALE%7CA380142689&v=2.1&u=ucalgary&it=r&p=AONE&sw=w&asid=fe49330d1b4028a40b7c76c2d032063f

Grande, Sandy. (2014). See the forest and think like a mountain. In L. Reynolds (Ed.), *Imagine it better: Visions of what school might be* (pp. 14–20). Heinemann.

Hargreaves, Andy. (2014). Imagine the end of ranking. In L. Reynolds (Ed.), *Imagine it better: Visions of what school might be* (8-13). Portsmouth, NH: Heinemann.

ISTE Standards. (2016). *ISTE Standards for Teachers* (2nd ed.). ISTE (International Society for Technology in Education). Retrieved from http://www.iste.org/standards/standards/for-educators

Johnson, L., Adams Becker, S., Estrada, V., & Freeman, A. (2016). *NMC Horizon report: 2016 K-12 edition*. Austin, TX: The New Media Consortium.

Manitoba Education. (2016). *Literacy with ICT across the curriculum: A model for 21st century learning from K-12*. Retrieved from http://www.edu.gov.mb.ca/k12/tech/lict/

Plair, S. K. (2007). Revamping professional development for technology integration and fluency. *The Clearing House: A Journal of Educational Strategies, Issues and Ideas, 82*(2), 70-74.

Thomas, D., & Brown, J. S. (2011). *A new culture of learning: Cultivating the imagination for a world of constant change* (Vol. 219). Lexington, KY: CreateSpace.

UNESCO. (2008*). Competency standards for teachers: Policy framework*. Retrieved from http://unesdoc.unesco.org/images/0015/001562/156207e.pdf

Whitty, E., & Clarke, M. (2012). Irish mathematics teachers' attitudes towards inclusion. *European Journal of Special Needs Education*, 27(2), 237-256.

About the Author
Will Burton is currently a Grade 10 Advisor at Maples Met School. He was born into a farming family in the United Kingdom before moving to rural Manitoba in the early 2000s. Will has been teaching in Winnipeg since 2013 at the elementary and high-school level. He is currently working on his thesis for a Master's in Education for Sustainable Development and Well-being from the University of Manitoba.

Who Should Read This Chapter?
Readers interested in a framework that grounds and focuses education for environment, along with a project-based learning unit case study as an exemplar.

The Theme of This Chapter in Three Phrases
Environmentalism; Earth Charter; case study.

As an Educator, What Are You Passionate About?
Playing a role in transforming an education system to one that supports the reconnection between humans and the environment, and developing sequential learning plans that link learners with experts and authentic experiences in the community.

CHAPTER 10
Ecological Literacy and Project-Based Learning

Will Burton, Maples Met School
Winnipeg, Manitoba, Canada

In Annie Proulx's 2016 novel *Barkskins,* she details the history of two families dating back to the 17th century. The first family, the Sels, were Mi'kmaq from the northeast coast of Turtle Island; the second, the Duquets, later known as the Dukes, are settlers of French descent in modern-day Quebec. The book traces both families' relationship to the continent's vast woodland. Initially, the Duquets seek to wield control over the woodland purely to survive in the perceived hostile environment. Later, as this control becomes stronger with the harnessing of technology, the Duquets move to harvesting the woodland to build their fortune, chopping and slicing the trees before selling. Conversely, Proulx writes that the Sels have lived off the land for generations, using the woodland for hunting and pulling select plant species for medicinal purposes. As the story moves forward, European domination of the ecosystem increases and the forest is culled, and the Sels begin to lose the balance they have with nature, forcing them to leave their traditional way of life and join the Europeans as they deplete the forest.

Barkskins offers us a story often repeated with variations around the world. Colonialism and the dominance of white, Western-European capitalism might well have sown the seeds for the comforts that we enjoy today, but it has come at an incredible cost to our planet. I have little doubt that we are aware of our complicity in this destruction. Yet here we are participating in the cyclical and growing devastation of Planet Earth.

Where we are as educators today is a result of historical and political forces. In this chapter I hope to draw connections between the widening duality between much of humankind and the natural world, particularly in Western capitalist societies, and the impact that this disconnect has on our understanding, preservation, and restoration of Planet Earth. My central thesis is that education should play a key role in reconnecting humans with the biosphere. Working toward this goal, I will explore how the United Nations Earth Charter, when employed through a project-based and integrative subject learning framework, can offer a way for educators to make deeper connections in their learning spaces (both indoor and outdoor). I'll conclude with a case study I was involved in that aimed to bring alive these theoretical considerations.

Duality: Humankind and the Natural World

The emerging duality between humankind and the planet can be traced back to the writings of René Descartes in the 17th century. Pepper (1996) begins his discussion of the emergence of the Anthropocene with Descartes, a philosopher who viewed mind and matter as separate entities. Humans, Descartes believed, were separate from the rest of the natural world because they possessed a soul, were self-reflective, were able to think rationally, and contemplated the results of their actions. The rest of nature, including animals, was machine-like and reactive; therefore, Descartes maintained, *homo sapiens* should not concern themselves with how they treated other species (Pepper, 1996, p. 53). While Descartes did not directly call for human domination over nature, Bai (2015) considers his philosophy one with which we can draw a line connecting today's binary view of human/nature (Bai, 2015, p. 137). What we have at present in North America and Europe is a duality between humankind and the natural world (Howell & Passmore, 2013, p. 231). Whereas once humans lived in a symbiotic relationship with their natural environment, today we harness our planet for our own needs and desires.

Margaret Atwood has explored the connection between humankind and nature in *Survival: A Thematic Guide to Canadian Literature* (1972). In a colonial context, Atwood suggested, survival in Canada pitted nature against humans: the former with its rugged, unforgiving, and extreme character versus the latter, a determined yet naive European settler. We can see this played out in *Barkskins*. Of Canadian identity, Atwood states that "we need such a map desperately.... we need to know about here, because here is where we live. For members of a country or a culture, shared knowledge of their place, their here, is not a luxury but a necessity. Without that knowledge we will not survive" (p. 19).

From the perspective of human knowledge, separating spaces, objects, and actions helped organize the world. The ever-widening horizons of human knowledge required categorization in an effort to understand and survive. For example, we might think, "When I go here, I expect to see this," and "When I see this person, I act this way." Eighteenth-century Swedish scientist Carl Linnaeus understood this, and around a century after Descartes he proposed that we separate humans from the natural world, thus elevating them. Linnaeus formalized an organizational system for plants and animals. His work laid the foundations for a binomial system of classification that denotes genus and species names. Even today his ideas allow zoologists and botanists to communicate through language barriers (Cleveland-Peck, 2007, p. 2).

While the categorization and classification of the natural world has played a role in the expansion of humankind's knowledge, it has not resulted in widespread respect for nature or a common belief in sustainable living. On the contrary, as threaded throughout the plot of *Barkskins*, settlers on this tract of North American land have become more and more successful at "surviving" by asserting dominance over the land.

Environmentalists have lamented the expanding gulf between populations and the natural environment. Goleman, Bennet, and Barlow (2012) point out that, as the majority of the world's population now lives in urban areas, it is even easier to ignore the myriad ways that the planet sustains us because today "our use of resources and the ensuing ecological impacts are dispersed across the entire planet – often seeming invisible or too far away for us to fully recognize" (Goleman, 2012, p. 5). The perceived temporal and geographical gulf between humans and that which is consumed means "most of us do not truly grasp how our everyday actions – our engagement in the systems of energy, agriculture, industry, commerce, and transportation on which we rely – can threaten the health and well-being of the earth" (Goleman, 2012, p. 4). The separation that exists makes it easier for humans to ignore the effects of our decisions on the planet. Heinberg (2010), citing Ornstein and Ehrlich (1989), claims the human brain is hard-wired for fight-or-flight responses to immediate danger, but is innately unable to effectively respond to slowly developing problems that are not personalized (Heinberg, 2010, p. 128). At present our earthly existence is analogous to the frog in the saucepan: if the frog was dropped in with the water already boiling, it would jump out, but the frog will boil alive in the pot if the temperature rises gradually.

The gradual transformation of the humankind/nature relationship leads us to the present day, where families no longer need to stock up on food for the winter months because they can visit Safeway in December for strawberries from elsewhere. Likewise, accurate reading of animal behaviour and cloud patterns has been replaced by a weather app on our phone. Generations ago, people migrated annually to find a food source, whereas today people may migrate for a better job or standard of living. Research has made clear that our widening proximity to the knowledge for sustaining our body continues to result in reduced ecological knowledge of our natural environment (Berry, 2007, p. 107), as well as less respect for the natural environment (Naess, 2005, p. 516) and physical and mental damage to our minds and bodies (Louv, 2008, p. 108). Yet, as Noddings (2003) reminds us, "there is evidence that a connection between people and nature, beyond the need for food, is inherently necessary.... human beings have a genetically based need to affiliate with nature" (Noddings, 2003, p. 124).

Planetary Crisis

Whether it be widespread species loss (the focus of Elizabeth Kolbert's 2014 book *Sixth Extinction*), climate change that is heating up the planet (resulting in extreme weather events, areas no longer able to sustain human life, and the melting of polar ice that will raise sea levels), or the exploitation of natural resources, driven both by both rampant capitalist consumerism in the developed world and a response to global inequality in the developing world, our planet and the human life currently residing on it is facing multiple crises. Johann Rockström (2010) of the Stockholm Resilience Centre speaks of the challenges we face from climate change in terms of "planetary boundaries." Rockström states that there is mounting evidence that we are "crossing hard-wired thresholds at the planetary level, threatening the self-regulating capacity of the planet to remain in the stable and favourable state in which human civilizations and societies have developed during the past 10,000 years" (Rockström, 2010, p. 72).

With his colleagues, Rockström outlines nine critical earth-system processes, including climate change, depletion of stratospheric ozone, land-use change, freshwater use, rate of biological diversity loss, ocean acidification, amounts of nitrogen and phosphorus inputs to the biosphere and oceans, air pollution from aerosol loading, and chemical pollution (p. 73). These systems are not closed loops, but work with and support each other, meaning that if one system exceeds its capacity and fails, then it no longer has the ability to support other systems. If we are able to stay within the capacity limits of these nine systems, then humankind can buy time to reduce the burden on them (p. 74). The latest report in 2015 from the group studying the planetary boundaries found that the limits of biogeochemical, land-system, and climate change were either in the zone of uncertainty (increasing risk) or beyond the zone of uncertainty (high risk) for surpassing the capacity of the system (Steffen et al., 2015, p. 6).

On the Canadian prairies where I currently live, we will not be immune to these coming changes. Whereas the current benefits of a cold winter include recreation, northern transportation over frozen ground, fewer pests, and an abundant and reliable source of water from melting snow (Diaz, Kulshreshtha, & Sauchyn, 2010, p. 356), researcher David Schindler, writing in 2010, stated:

> Positive effects of the warming will be few, and disadvantages many. Agriculture will be much diminished, with the advantages of a warmer and longer growing season more than offset by a lack of water. Prairie forest boundaries will be pushed far to the north, largely the result of increased fires, some following extensive insect outbreaks. Precipitation events will be fewer, but more intense. Transportation by water, and tourism and recreation on water resources, will be almost non-existent (Diaz, Kulshreshtha, & Sauchyn, 2010, p. x).

These are not purely environmental ramifications; the effects will hit the economy. Indeed, we are beginning to see these changes play out in Manitoba, with the melting of permafrost causing damage to the railway line connecting southern Manitoba with the northern Manitoba community of Churchill.

Blair Feltmate is an associate professor in the School of Environment, Enterprise and Development at the University of Waterloo. In summer 2017, he was appointed by the Canadian government to chair an expert panel on preparing Canadians for the challenges of climate change. When interviewed by CBC's Aaron Wherry, he argued that at present Canadians are not well prepared for a changing climate. With each new disaster, more and more citizens and politicians are behind efforts in allocating resources and preparation, but he is concerned that we are not evolving fast enough. "We do not have the luxury of time," he states. "We've got to get on with adaptation." Feltmate outlined that for Canadians to become prepared requires two steps: reducing emissions, and preparing communities and individuals to deal with the unavoidable consequences of climate change (Wherry, 2017). Education can play a pivotal role in both of these steps.

Education and the Environment

So, to summarize: the divide between humans and the natural world has been widening, particularly in the West. This division has led to a lack of understanding and respect for the natural world. Humans have an inherent biological connection to nature, but through the dualism that started with Descartes and Linnaeus, and accelerated with technological innovation, we are now at a point where multiple planetary boundaries are being crossed, with massive ramifications for the natural world and human life within it.

What role has education played in the relationship between humans and the natural environment? What might be done to reverse our current trajectory? The divide between humankind and the biosphere was replicated in the development and spread of modern Western education. Thirty years ago, the renowned ecologist Arne Naess called for "a more ecocentric ethic … embracing plants and animals as well as people, is required for human societies to live in harmony with the natural world on which they depend for their survival and well-being" (Payne & Newman, 2005, pp. 241-242). Key to my discussion, however, is what Naess followed these comments with, stating:

> Such an ethic would surely be more effective if it were acted upon by people who believe in its validity, rather than merely its usefulness. This, I think, will come to be understood more and more by those in charge of educational policies. Quite simply, it is indecent for a teacher to proclaim an ethic for tactical reasons only (Payne & Newman, 2005, p. 242).

Today, educational scholars are represented in the chorus of thinkers calling for changes to the way humans interact with the planet. Academics such as David Orr (1994), Daniel Goleman (2012), Richard Kahn (2010), Moacir Gadotti (2010), and the late Paulo Freire (2004) have written reams of pages on the inadequacy of current approaches to public education and the imperative that changes be made in order to address the environmental question. These changes are specific to two areas: content and structure of the school day.

Chet Bowers has emerged as one of North America's foremost critics of contemporary public education, writing extensively on both content and structure in public education. Indeed, all texts written in Bowers' career since the mid-1980s are founded in the reform of public education for ecoliteracy, a conscious commitment to the environmental crisis, and an ideal that Bowers terms "recovering the ecological imperative" (Bowers, 2003, p. xi). Since then Bowers has investigated the connection between ecological devastation and atomization in society (Bowers, 2012, p. 302), reliance on technology (Bowers, 2003, p. 3), and language (Bowers, 2003, p. xi), and has called for looking to Indigenous populations as a source of guidance for navigating away from the era of the Anthropocene (Bowers, 1987, p. 158). Bowers outlines his perspective on contemporary education's connection to the environment most fully in *Culture of Denial* (1997). Here he states:

> [It is] increasingly difficult to ignore the connections between the high-status forms of knowledge promoted by public schools and universities and the ecological crisis.... Few public school teachers and university professors recognize how modern values and behavioural patterns are connected to the ecological crisis, [and] it will become increasingly necessary for environmentally conscious groups to challenge what is being taught in our educational institutions (Bowers, 1997, p. 1-2).

Unless we make a change in the content and delivery of information, Bowers warns that "there will be an unending series of environmental problems that will keep attention focused on the immediate consequences of these cultural beliefs and practices, and not on the source of the problem" (Bowers, 1997, p. 18).

Another prominent thinker, D.W. Orr (1994), states that educators can play a key role in environmental conservation, believing that they themselves "must become students of the ecologically proficient mind and of the things that must be done to foster such minds" (Orr, 1994, p. 3). Orr believes that we are continuing to educate as if there is no planetary crisis, placing instead blind faith in technology to save us (p. 2). Likewise, Jacobson, McDuff, and Monroe (2006) state that "people are part of the problem and public education will be part of the solution.... [C]onservation education and outreach programs are a critical component in changing course toward a more sustainable future" (p. 1).

Moving from a macro- to micro-analysis of challenges in teaching environmental education, a literature review of research conducted on education for sustainable development in Manitoba over the last 16 years leads to three central conclusions. First, the siloing of subjects (teaching language arts, science, social studies, and mathematics separately) prevents effective teaching for environmental education (Hart (2002), Metz et al. (2010), Belton (2013), Kraljevic (2011), Jacques (2012), Eckton (2016), Babiuk & Falkenberg (2010)); second, many educators found that either an overcrowded curriculum or an overly restrictive curriculum creates a challenging environment for effective teaching of environmental education (Hart (2002), Metz et al. (2010), Jacques (2012), Eckton (2016), Belton (2013), Michalos et al. (2015), Babiuk & Falkenberg (2010)); third, these two elements working together have not led to strong knowledge or positive behaviours in relation to the environment.

The United Nations and the Earth Charter

Education therefore is a problem and a solution, a view shared by the United Nations. In 1987, the international organization released *Our Common Future*, better known as the Brundtland Report. As with the work of the aforementioned academics, the Brundtland Report identified education as a key component in developing "changes in attitudes, in social values, and in aspirations" (United Nations, 1987, n.p.). Alongside nongovernmental organizations and the scientific community, educational institutions, it argued, "will play a crucial part in putting the world onto sustainable development paths, in laying the groundwork for *Our Common Future*" (United Nations, 1987, n.p.). These institutions are crucial to supporting citizens in becoming more skillful, productive, and better problem solvers, and can work toward these aims by being relevant to local conditions, including knowledge of soils, water, and deforestation, and supportive in how the community and the individual can reverse environmental destruction (United Nations, 1987, n.p.). The Brundtland Report called for environmental education to "be included in and should run throughout the other disciplines of the formal education curriculum at all levels – to foster a sense of responsibility for the state of the environment and to teach students how to monitor, protect, and improve it" (United Nations, 1987, n.p.).

Our Common Future went on to cite the importance of taking a localized approach to changing systems of education, with learning in theoretical and practical experiences. An environmentally conscious student must have hard skills and knowledge in management of local resources, such as local soils and water – not just their conservation but the regeneration of depleted or damaged resources – and soft skills in creative, productive problem solving (United Nations, 1987, n.p.). To meet these ends, education institutions need to ensure that learning for sustainable development draws together and cuts across the social and natural sciences and the humanities, "thus providing insights on the interaction between natural and human resources, between development and environment" (United Nations, 1987, n.p.). As echoed by educational theorists, moving away from the siloing of subject and content areas and instead integrating subject areas in an effort to cultivate holistic environmental understanding is essential.

Project-based learning promises to provide an opportunity to meet these demands. Drawing together subject areas into a single temporal space, and employing environmental content as the foundation for students to develop questions and pursue answers that are complex, requires the connection of traditionally distinct subject-knowledge areas. For example, a student may decide to ask "How can I increase active transportation to school?" as an essential question. Answering this question may require them to conduct interviews with students, families, and community members, and research areas such as city planning and governance, active living, human psychology, poverty, fossil-fuel consumption, and population distribution, to name but a few. Subject areas connected with environmental content could include English language arts, science, mathematics, history, geography, health, civics, and global issues. The pooling of subjects into larger blocks of time provides multiple advantages. Firstly, students can leave the school and get out into the community for field experiences or to hear from experts, often referred to as "leaving to learn." Secondly, the larger blocks of time allow for instructional, work, and support time so that students can immerse themselves in the project work.

To support educators in cultivating their learning environments, a framework of common knowledge, understandings, and principles was published by the United Nations to encapsulate the educational philosophy of *Our Common Future*. Created by an independent commission of the United Nations following the 1992 Rio Earth Summit, the Earth Charter was the result of an extensive decade-long consultation process with over five thousand individuals, including scientists, government, students, Indigenous groups, and grassroots communities (Clugston et al., 2002, p. 2). This consultation culminated in a "a global consensus statement of values and principles for a sustainable future," and a call for unity "to bring forth a sustainable global society founded on respect for nature, universal human rights, economic justice, and a culture of peace" (Earth Charter, 2000, n.d.). Since its release, the Charter has been endorsed by thousands of organizations, including UNESCO and the World Conservation Union.

The premise of the Earth Charter, according to Clugston et al. (2002), is that at present many societies around the world are unsustainable, and humanity as a whole is responsible for environmental degradation and climate change. The document holds that education must play a central role in making the transition to sustainability (Clugston et al., in Leal Filho, 2002, p. 6).

The Charter is divided into four sections and sixteen principles:

Section	Principles
1. Respect and Care for the Community of Life	▪ Respect Earth and life in all its diversity. ▪ Care for the community of life with understanding, compassion, and love. ▪ Build democratic societies that are just, participatory, sustainable, and peaceful. ▪ Secure Earth's bounty and beauty for present and future generations
2. Ecological Integrity	▪ Protect and restore the integrity of Earth's ecological systems, with special concern for biological diversity and the natural processes that sustain life. ▪ Prevent harm as the best method of environmental protection and, when knowledge is limited, apply a precautionary approach. ▪ Adopt patterns of production, consumption, and reproduction that safeguard Earth's regenerative capacities, human rights, and community well-being. ▪ Advance the study of ecological sustainability and promote the open exchange and wide application of the knowledge acquired.

Section	Principles
3. Social and Economic Justice	■ Eradicate poverty as an ethical, social, and environmental imperative. ■ Ensure that economic activities and institutions at all levels promote human development in an equitable and sustainable manner. ■ Affirm gender equality and equity as prerequisites to sustainable development and ensure universal access to education, health care, and economic opportunity. ■ Uphold the right of all, without discrimination, to a natural and social environment supportive of human dignity, bodily health, and spiritual well-being, with special attention to the rights of Indigenous peoples and minorities.
4. Democracy, Nonviolence, and Peace	■ Strengthen democratic institutions at all levels, and provide transparency and accountability in governance, inclusive participation in decision making, and access to justice. ■ Integrate into formal education and life-long learning the knowledge, values, and skills needed for a sustainable way of life. ■ Treat all living beings with respect and consideration. ■ Promote a culture of tolerance, nonviolence, and peace.

(United Nations, The Earth Charter, 2000b)

The Earth Charter has been considered by critical theorists such as Richard Kahn, Moacir Gadotti, and Richard Clugston as a valuable benchmark from which to orient environmental education. Clugston et al. (2002) declares it a "potent force for change in the way we think about the Earth and ourselves" (p. 2). In outlining how educators might utilize the Earth Charter in their practice, the authors identify two roles: first, as a framework and source of content for education for sustainable living and, second, as a catalyst for promoting an ongoing multisectional dialogue on global ethics (p. 4). In other words, the Earth Charter blends education for sustainable living with a critical perspective on contemporary society.

Gruenewald (2004) laments the defanging of environmental education, a discipline he contends began with the aim of transforming education, but through its institutionalization has lost all meaning and should be abolished (p. 72). Instead, he points to the Earth Charter as an example of what should replace it – a document that "is able to negotiate the complex ecological interactions between science, politics, and culture, between social and ecological systems, and their impact on human and nonhuman life" (p. 94). Gruenewald maintains that the Earth Charter carries weight because of the thousands of valid contributors, and that its development was backed and continues to be promoted by the United Nations. Further, the document

> succinctly expresses the interrelated social and ecological crises facing humanity in four principal areas—respect and care for the community of life, social and economic justice, ecological integrity, and democracy, nonviolence, and peace—and outlines a response to these crises that has theoretical and practical relevance (p. 96).

The Earth Charter challenges free-market capitalism and questions economic globalization, seeing the root of climate change and ecological devastation as the result of "local and global economic development patterns that are also at the root of injustice, poverty, violence, and oppression" (p. 96). The critical perspective of our current economic structure provides a powerful context for learners to challenge the status quo and taken-for-granted practices as a foundation for taking action.

As documented by the United Nations in *Good Practices in Education for Sustainable Development Using the Earth Charter* (2007), the principles have been and continue to be adopted by K–12, postsecondary, and nonformal educational organizations as a framework for their pedagogy. Gruenewald (2004) sees the Earth Charter as a statement of specific standards by which educational policy can be evaluated (p. 97). Likewise, Sauer (2002) calls it "a statement of standards by which people may measure progress toward a just and sustainable society."

Like these educational thinkers, I believe that the Earth Charter can provide a valuable guide to supporting and focusing efforts in the classroom in a way that situates environmental education as the foundation of project-based learning. Recently, I was involved in a collaborative project that sought to implement the principles of the Earth Charter in a project-based learning school, of which I will now provide a brief overview and analysis.

Case Study: Maples Met School Water Conference

In 2017–2018, grade 10 students from Maples Met School in Winnipeg, Canada, collaborated on a semester-long series of experiences, research, and workshops devoted to scientific knowledge and social issues about water. Students immersed themselves in learning through a variety of mediums, and were tasked with developing research and/or a workshop. Grade 10 students hosted more than 400 grade 8 students from Seven Oaks School Division at Maples Collegiate at a Water Conference on January 19th, 2018.

A series of learning experiences designed to provide a variety of practice and theory were organized throughout the semester to enhance students' understanding of the importance of water to ecosystems, with an emphasis placed on issues affecting Manitoba.

September 18, 2017: Water Project Kickoff, Oak Hammock Marsh
All grade 10 students visited Oak Hammock Marsh. For the first half of the day, students heard from three organizations: Lake Winnipeg Foundation on the current state of Lake Winnipeg, Green Action Centre on water usage and waste, and Ducks Unlimited on invasive water species. For the second half of the day, students went out on a marsh walk in the Oak Hammock area, where they identified animal and plant life, and undertook invertebrate sampling from the marsh.

September 25 and 26, 2017: Experimental Lakes Area Visit
All grade 10 students visited the Experimental Lakes Area (ELA) for an overnight trip. Students were guided by the scientists at ELA through a series of procedures concerning eutrophication, climate-change data, fish tagging, and nanosilver, along with use of a chemistry lab and a meteorology station and connections to service learning. Students spent the night at the ELA site and were immersed in the work of the organization.

October 5, 2017: Freshwater Ecology Day, Fort Whyte Alive
A select group of students needing additional support in building their knowledge and scientific competency, or with a research project specific to issues of clean water, attended Fort Whyte Alive, an environmental education centre, for the day. Topics covered included drainage in the Lake Winnipeg watershed, invertebrates and zooplankton, water monitoring, water chemistry, Indigenous water teachings, and citizen science.

October 11, 2017: Water Testing with Fort Whyte Alive
A facilitator from Fort Whyte Alive visited Maples Met School and worked with grade 10 students on water-testing procedures. Students visited a water-retention pond in the local community, took samples, and worked through a series of testing procedures to identify the quality of the water and environmental concerns that might have an impact.

October 18, 2017: Site Visit at Red River at Kildonan Park, The Forks
All grade 10 Maples Met students visited two sites outside of the Maples community where they conducted an environmental scan and collected water samples. Students observed human interaction with the water, and collected data on animal and plant life. Students were exposed to historical events connected to the location.

November, 2017: Class reading of Aqueduct *(2016)*
Students undertook a reading of *Aqueduct: Colonialism, Resources, and the Histories We Remember*, a book by University of Manitoba history professor Adele Perry. The text highlighted the historical significance of the Winnipeg aqueduct, its importance to the development of Winnipeg as a city, and the huge impact that the aqueduct had on the Indigenous peoples (Anishinaabe) of Shoal Lake 40 (the site of Winnipeg's water supply).

November 2017 to January 2018: Water Workshop Project Development
Between November and late December, grade 10 students at Maples Met School focused their project work on experiments and research related to water issues. They were asked to develop a workshop, present research findings, and develop a workshop component. The students geared their work toward meeting both grade 10 and grade 8 curriculum learning outcomes.

January 19, 2018: Water Conference, Maples Collegiate
Grade 10 students hosted an all-day Water Conference at Maples Collegiate for all grade 8 students in Seven Oaks School Division. The day was opened by Indigenous activist Clayton Thomas-Müller, who spoke about his work as a water protector at the Standing Rock protest against the Dakota Access pipeline. The 400-plus grade 8 students were split into 16 groups, and attended between three and five workshops in an afternoon of breakout sessions. The

workshops included conducting experiments, viewing poster boards, watching presentations, and viewing videos developed by students. All presentations were interactive and lasted between 15 and 45 minutes.

Our Water Conference initiative had multiple goals. First, we sought to provide a schema from which students could delve into rigorous and authentic research projects of their own choosing, within the constraint that it needed to connect in some way to issues or knowledge about water. The schema was founded in a series of experiential learning opportunities, where students heard and worked with experts in the community. Each advisor worked independently with students to connect their interests with a project they were passionate about. Following this, project proposals were posted on an online project-based learning platform called "Project Foundry" that allowed them to directly connect the grade 10 learning outcomes from all subject areas to their project work. This process allowed the student to take ownership of their project's curricula connections. Students developed task lists, and advisors set deadlines for a presentation of research and a dry run of the workshops (which took place three weeks before the Water Conference).

The multitude of human and environmental connections to water led to a breadth of projects. These included work on the eradication of blue-green algae from Lake Winnipeg, the use of aquaponics systems to grow food at home, the role of colonialism in preventing the Indigenous community of Shoal Lake 40 from accessing clean drinking water, awareness campaigns on invasive species of fish, reducing water waste in the home, how coastal cities are preparing for rising sea levels, and the environmental impact of purchasing bottled water. Key to the success of these projects was that students had the autonomy to select a research project that they were passionate about, meaning that their curiosity fed into a desire to undertake research projects of quality.

Second, we set an expectation that students would need to showcase their research through a workshop which would be hosted during the Water Conference. The understanding that there would be a public demonstration of their learning meant they had a goal and deadline to work toward. All students in grade 10 knew that they were part of a community with a common objective. At our school we expect that projects result in a finished product. Within the conference framework, we outlined that they would need to develop a project that connected with curriculum outcomes, but that also required the production of an engaging workshop lasting no less than 15 minutes. Again, students were given the opportunity to decide the most effective way to engage their audience within those parameters.

Third, there was our drive to connect with the community. This was done in multiple ways. Our school hosted more than 400 grade 8 students from across the school division – youth who were potentially future Met School students themselves. By inviting them and their classroom teachers into our space, we were showcasing our school as an option for them in the following year, generating excitement about project-based learning, and placing value on environmental education. Stakeholders in the community, including superintendents, school-board trustees, and the Minister for Sustainable Development all attended, as did environmental educators from Manitoba Eco-Network, Lake Winnipeg Foundation, and Fort Whyte Alive. Our Divisional Elder Mary Courchene and keynote speaker Clayton Thomas Müller have Indigenous backgrounds, and that helped us from the outset to make strong connections between environmental education and reconciliation. The Water Conference was also featured in multiple local newspapers.

Were we successful in developing a cross-curricular framework within the project-based learning model? Without a doubt, yes. If we use the barometer of meeting cross-curricular outcomes, then all learners connected with multiple learning outcomes from the grade 10 English language arts, Reading is Thinking, science, and geography curriculums. Students' work was able to draw in mathematics, information computer technology, visual arts, food and nutrition, and career development as well. All student-driven questions, research, and workshops were powerful examples of rigorous and authentic learning.

Were we successful in drawing in the principles of the Earth Charter within a project-based learning framework? Over the course of the semester, including the foundational field experiences, projects, and workshops, almost all of the principles of the Earth Charter were identified in some manner. "Respect and Care for the Community of Life," "Ecological Integrity," "Social and Economic Justice" and "Democracy, Nonviolence, and Peace" were touched on in at least a handful of workshops, though biological diversity and direct consideration of the role of government and capitalism were less prevalent. As with all project-based learning, what these research projects offered was an opportunity for students to undertake deep research into specific areas at the cost of breadth of knowledge. This poses the challenge of developing a breadth of understanding, which the Earth Charter indicates we should work toward. While many students were involved in reviewing many workshops before the conference, in turn becoming exposed to the content, this would not be considered sufficient for determining that they clearly understood the material. Ultimately, in project-based learning, breadth of content and depth of content may be incompatible.

In addition, if we consider knowledge, attitude, and actions as three measures of ecological literacy, then this case study provides evidence of ecoliteracy growth in knowledge and attitudes, but not in actions. Shallcross (2005) has highlighted this as a major deficiency in the current practice of public education, which demands that students take on content knowledge about what positive actions an individual might take even as teachers do little to encourage or provide opportunities for action (Shallcross in Metz et al., 2010, p. 156). Kumler (2010) argues that even when action is undertaken, it is often tokenistic and rarely risks becoming meaningful (Kumler, 2010, p. 25). We might well ask ourselves what good knowledge or attitudes toward the environment are unless they are accompanied by actions. As Richard Kahn argues,

> Western critical literacy would doubtless involve taking action on [environmental] issues at both an individual and collective level, engaging with ecological and sustainable countercultures, rescuing animals and habitats whenever possible, and working for revolutionary counter-hegemonic social change generally in favor of abolishing civic hierarchies based on race, class, gender and other categories of identified social difference (Kahn in Darder, 2009, p. 533-534).

Knowledge and attitudes are often addressed and assessed in classrooms, but owing to curriculum, resource, time, or teacher knowledge constraints, students rarely put their ideas into action beyond the classroom walls. Indeed, accompanying positive attitudes toward the planet might be our biggest challenge as educators. Those educators who provide opportunities for action and orient their work around providing spaces for action are what Misiaszek (2016) calls "ecopedagogues." These educators aim for their "teaching to lead to action from learners ... which includes reflection about which actions need to be taken [and] often leads to re/questioning how to define the deeper structures of society which need to be transformed in order to lead to this better world" (Misiaszek, 2016, p. 590). In addition, ecopedagogues "focus on the politics behind environmentally harmful actions, the normative systems and structures of society guiding these actions, and the deeper, transformative steps needed to end these actions" (p. 590). What project-based learning offers is the opportunity to guide students' questions and research toward praxis in the community, which should be an end goal of all environmentally focused learning.

Conclusion

In this chapter, I have highlighted the duality that emerged between humankind and the natural environment over the last three centuries, and how that organization and categorization of knowledge has been replicated through public-education institutions. The need to reform education certainly lies beyond just responding to our current environmental crisis, but if you consider the current environmental crisis the most important issue facing humanity, then reform is all the more important. The United Nation's Earth Charter was provided as a potential framework that educators might look toward in an effort to inform their practice in the classroom, and the case study of Maples Met School's Water Conference is an exemplar of what drawing on these principles within a project-based learning environment might look like.

In the conclusion to *Barkskins*, Proulx writes of the Sel and Duquet families uniting in a joint effort to replant the forests that their ancestors destroyed, ending the book on a positive yet inconclusive note. Only through recognizing the missteps of history and working toward the common good might we be able to move beyond preservation toward restoration. Likewise in education. Stakeholders including parents, community members, and elected officials as well as teachers and students must work together to recognize that part of living a sustainable life on a healthy planet will need a reconceptualization of what education looks like. Integrating formerly distinct subject areas and grounding learning in a strong notion of the environment are two key steps toward meeting this objective. Project-based learning by itself is not the answer to our current educational and ecological crisis. But reimagining and actually reforming education with the values of sustainability in mind will need to draw on elements of project-based learning to be successful.

References

Antunes A., & Gadotti, M. (2006). Ecopedagogy as the appropriate pedagogy to the Earth Charter process. In P. Blaze, M. Vilela, & A. Roerink (Eds.), *The Earth Charter in action: Toward a sustainable development* (pp. 135-137). Amsterdam: Kit Publisher.

Atwood, M. (2012). *Survival: a thematic guide to Canadian literature*. Toronto: House of Anansi Press.

Babiuk, G., & Falkenberg. T. (2010). *Sustainable development and living through changing teacher education and teaching in Manitoba*. Winnipeg, MB: University of Manitoba.

Bai, H. (2015). Peace with the earth: Animism and contemplative ways. *Cultural Studies of Science Education, 10*, 135-147.

Belton, C. (2013). *Successes, drivers and barriers of education for sustainable development in Canada, England and Australia*. Winnipeg, MB : University of Manitoba.

Berry, W., & Grubbs, M. A. (2007). *Conversations with Wendell Berry*. Jackson, MS: University Press of Mississippi.

Bowers, C. A. (1997). *The culture of denial: Why the environmental movement needs a strategy for reforming universities and public schools*. Albany, NY: State University of New York Press.

———(2003). *Mindful conservatism: Rethinking the ideological and educational basis of an ecologically sustainable future*. Lanham, MD: Rowman & Littlefield Publishers.

Cleveland-Peck, Patricia. (2007). Garden of Sweden. *History Today, 57*(5), 2-3.

Diaz, H. P., Kulshreshtha, S. N., & Sauchyn, D. J. (2010). *The new normal: the Canadian prairies in a changing climate*. Regina, SK: University of Regina Press.

Eckton, H. M. (2016). *Education for sustainable living: Exploring the landscape of one urban high school's sustainability practices and values*. Winnipeg, MB: University of Manitoba.

Freire, P. (2004). *Pedagogy of indignation*. Boulder, CO: Paradigm Publishers.

Gadotti, M. (2010). Reorienting education practices toward sustainability. *Journal of Education for Sustainable Development, 4*(2), 203-211.

Goleman, D., Bennett, L., & Barlow, Z. (2012). *Ecoliterate: How educators are cultivating emotional, social, and ecological intelligence* (1st ed.). San Francisco, CA: Jossey-Bass.

Gruenewald, D. A. (2004). A Foucauldian analysis of environmental education: Toward the socioecological challenge of the Earth Charter. *Curriculum Inquiry, 34*(1), 71-107.

Hart, P. (2002). Environment in the science curriculum: The politics of change in the Pan-Canadian science curriculum development process. *International Journal of Science Education, 24*(11), 1239-1254.

Heinberg, R. (2010). *Peak everything: Waking up to the century of declines*. Gabriola Island, BC: New Society Publishers.

Henderson, M. (2016). *Bridging the ecological knowledge and knowledge-action gaps: A utopian vision for education in Manitoba*. Winnipeg, MB: University of Manitoba.

Howell, A. J., & Passmore, H.-A. (2013). The nature of happiness: Nature affiliation and mental well-being. In C. L. M. Keyes (Ed.), *Mental well-being: International contributions to the study of positive mental health* (pp. 231-257). New York, NY: Springer.

Jacques, C. (2012). *The green Don Quixotes: Values development of education for sustainable development teachers*. Winnipeg, MB: University of Manitoba.

Kahn, R. V. (2010). *Critical pedagogy, ecoliteracy, & planetary crisis: The ecopedagogy movement*. New York, NY: Peter Lang.

Kolbert, E. (2014). *The sixth extinction: An unnatural history*. London: Bloomsbury.

Kraljevic, G. M. (2011). *Does the Manitoba science curriculum help teach teens to be more environmentally-minded?* Winnipeg, MB: University of Manitoba.

Leal Filho, W. (2002). *Teaching sustainability at universities: Toward curriculum greening*. New York, NY: Peter Lang.

Louv, R. (2008). *Last child in the woods: Saving our children from nature-deficit disorder* (Updated and expanded). Chapel Hill, NC: Algonquin Books.

McKeown, R., & Nolet, V. (Eds.). (2013). *Schooling for sustainable development in Canada and the United States*. New York, NY: Springer.

Metz, D., McMillan, B., Maxwell, M., & Tetrault, A. (2010). Securing the place of educating for sustainable development within existing curriculum frameworks: A reflective analysis. *Canadian Journal of Environmental Education, 15*, 150-169.

Michalos, A., Kahlke, P., Rempel, K., Lounatvuori, A., MacDiarmid, A., Creech, H., & Buckler, C. (2015). Progress in measuring knowledge, attitudes and behaviours concerning sustainable development among tenth grade students in Manitoba. *An International and Interdisciplinary Journal for Quality-of-Life Measurement, 123*(2), 303-336.

Misiaszek, G. W. (2015). Ecopedagogy and citizenship in the age of globalisation: Connections between environmental and global citizenship education to save the planet. *European Journal of Education, 50*(3), 280-292.

Newman, R. S., & Payne, D. G. (Eds.). (2005). *The Palgrave environmental reader*. New York, NY: Palgrave Macmillan.

Noddings, N. (2003). *Happiness and education*. Cambridge, UK: Cambridge University Press.

Ornstein, R. E., & Ehrlich, P. R. (1989). *New world new mind: Moving toward conscious evolution*. New York, NY: Doubleday.

Orr, D. W. (1994). *Earth in mind: On education, environment, and the human prospect*. Washington, DC: Island Press.

Pepper, D. (1996). *Modern environmentalism: An introduction*. London: Routledge.

Proulx, A. (2016). *Barkskins: A novel*. New York, NY: Scribner.

Rockström, J. (2010). Planetary boundaries. *New Perspectives Quarterly, 27*(1), 72-74.

Sauer, P. (n.d.). Global ethics: An American perspective. *Orion Magazine*. Retrieved from https://orionmagazine.org/article/global-ethics-an-american-perspective/

Steffen, W., Richardson, K., Rockström, J., Cornell, S. E., Fetzer, I., Bennett, E. M., Sörlin, S. (2015, February 13). Sustainability. Planetary boundaries: guiding human development on a changing planet. *Science, 347*(6223), 1259855.

United Nations (Ed.). (2000a). What is the Earth Charter? Retrieved from http://earthcharter.org/discover/what-is-the-earth-charter/

———. (2000b). The Earth Charter. Retrieved from discover/the-earth-charter/

Wherry A. (2017, September 3). "We are not well prepared": An expert's view of climate change and the next big storm. *CBC News*. Retrieved from http://www.cbc.ca/news/politics/climate- change-adaptation-expert-panel-analysis-wherry-1.4271699

World Commission on Environment and Development. (1987). *Our common future*. Oxford: Oxford University Press.

About the Authors

Dr. Alex Wilson, Opaskwayak Cree Nation, is one of many organizers with the Idle No More movement, integrating progressive movement work with grassroots interventions that prevent the destruction of land and water. She is particularly focused on educating about and protecting the Saskatchewan River Delta and supporting community-based food sovereignty efforts. She is a full professor and the Academic Director at the Aboriginal Education Research Centre at the University of Saskatchewan.

Jacob Mans is a practicing architect and educator. His research is focused on understanding the relationship between landscape and building performance. Jacob holds a Bachelor of Arts degree in studio art from Luther College, a Master of Architecture degree from the University of Cincinnati, and a Master of Design Studies degree from Harvard University. He is a cofounder of the Decentralized Design Lab and an assistant professor of Architecture at the University of Minnesota.

Who Should Read This Chapter?

Educators, high-school and postsecondary students, graduate-level students, designers, architects, builders, environmentalists, researchers, Indigenous people, general public, activists, people interested in housing, land defenders.

The Theme of This Chapter in Three Phrases

Whole-community project-based learning, decolonization, and addressing the needs of community.

As Educators, What Are You Passionate About?

Social justice, anti-oppression education, land-based education, decolonization, protecting Indigenous lands and water, sustainability, teaching about architectural design beyond buildings within the larger environment.

CHAPTER 11

One House Many Nations: Indigenous Project-Based Collaboration

Alex Wilson, University of Saskatchewan, and Jacob Mans, University of Minnesota

When Idle No More[1] co-founder Sylvia McAdam was running for chief in her home nation of Big River, Saskatchewan, as she went door to door she became increasingly appalled by the living conditions of many of her fellow community members (Hyslop, 2017). At that time, she connected with other Idle No More organizers who recognized the same issues in their own communities. They then made the commitment to take action, first, by launching an educational campaign and, second, by building one house[2]. Although none had experience in home building, they were able to tap into the vast network of supporters and found a prairie-owned-and-operated company

---

1 Late in the fall of 2012, four women came together in Saskatchewan to respond to proposed legislation in Canada (Bills C-38 and C-45) that would erode environmental protection and affect the Treaty and human rights of Indigenous peoples (Gilio-Whitaker, 2015; McLean, 2014; Wilson, 2015; Wilson & Pilar, 2018). The women quickly mobilized a local network to organize land-defence actions, teach-ins, and informational campaigns to educate the community about the potential impact of the pending legislation. The movement, known as Idle No More (INM), spread across the prairie provinces and beyond, becoming the first global Indigenous movement in history (Woons, 2013). The authors would like to acknowledge the many people who have contributed and continue to contribute to the One House Many Nations campaign and the OCN sustainable village project.
2 The historian Adele Perry has helped to excavate the colonial foundations of Indigenous peoples' present-day housing crisis. In an article entitled "From 'the hot-bed of vice' to the 'good and well-ordered Christian home': First Nations Housing and Reform in Nineteenth-Century British Columbia," Perry (2003) provided a convincing argument that the forced resettlement of Indigenous people into villages, the reorganization of their communities, and the reformation of their housing practices were instruments wielded by both missionaries and governments to impose, maintain, and extend their supervision and social control of Indigenous peoples (p. 595).

that built mini-homes. Idle No More launched a crowdfunding call and within days raised enough money to pay for building materials and transportation of the house to its new owner in Big River First Nation. More than three hundred people – activists, builders, and both Indigenous and non-Indigenous community members – contributed their expertise and time to help build the house, or donated money or supplies. Within three weeks, the house was built. The campaign was a huge success in many respects: it raised awareness about the housing crisis and failed Treaty promises; it pressured First Nations, local, provincial, and federal governments to address human-rights violations; and, most importantly, it provided shelter for a person.

One House Many Nations first build on Big River First Nation. *IDLE NO MORE*

We also learned some valuable lessons in the first build, which we brought into the second One House Many Nations project. People are eager to contribute but often do not know how; colonial economics (which resulted in the isolation of First Nations people on reserves located on small tracts of land within their traditional territories – land that the settler population saw the least economic potential in) have impoverished First Nations people and communities; sustainability needs to be a part of the solution; systemic issues (including, but not limited to, the availability of funding for First Nations housing and the inadequacy of much of the housing available to people living on reserve) need to be addressed alongside individuals' immediate need for shelter; and mini-homes are not the answer to housing needs of First Nation communities.

The Saskatchewan River Delta and the Opaskwayak Cree Nation

Opaskwayak Cree Nation (OCN) is located in northern Manitoba in the heart of the Saskatchewan River Delta. The delta, comprising river systems, peat-moss bogs, and northern boreal forest, is one of the largest and most complex ecosystems on the planet. Currently, this environment is in critical danger and is being deforested at a rate faster than the Amazon rainforest (Smith & Cheng,

Wood pile from old-growth boreal forest harvested in the traditional territory of Opaskwayak Cree Nation. The pile extends for nearly a kilometre and contains enough timber to build more than 3,500 homes, but instead will be chipped to make kraft paper that will be used to manufacture bags for products such as pet food or cement. *DDL*

2015). The effects of deforestation are felt by inhabitants of the region, many of whom rely on harvesting wild foods and other resources from the forest, and globally, as the northern boreal forest, which captures and stores atmospheric carbon, plays a significant role in slowing and mitigating climate change. The rate of alterations to the boreal forest and the continuing effects will determine the future health of this ecosystem and of the people living there (Gauthier, Bernier, Kuuluvainen, Shvidenko, & Schepaschenko, 2015).

Approximately 3200 Opaskwaya Inniniwak (Cree people) live on the OCN reserve and another 2500 live off-reserve. Many community members work for local schools, the First Nation, or outside agencies, and some rely on government assistance.

Historically, OCN had sustainable housing systems and food sources. Shelters were made out of locally available materials, such as willow, birch, and spruce, mud and moss, and, as in any population, varied widely, reflecting the materials available at the time and place they were constructed, the seasons, the location, and the builders' personal skills, abilities, and preferences. Families hunted, trapped, and gathered local foods, and each family kept a small garden in the summer. The housing system fit well with the local geography and allowed people to live off the land, travel, and visit in spaces that suited both mobility and the extended family structures of Opaskwaya Inniniwak. In the early 1900s, the settlement was forcibly moved from the south side of the Saskatchewan

Clear-cutting in the northern boreal forest. *VIRGINIA JOHNS*

River (an area with topsoil and adjacent to rich farmland) to the north side of the river. Although today the community is geographically large and scattered over a number of sites, all have a clay base and very little topsoil to support the growth of trees, food sources, or other plant life. The reservation pass system restricted hunting, trapping, and travel to sacred or significant sites. In the 1960s, the Grand Rapids hydro-dam project flooded traplines and seasonal homes and changed the migration patterns of birds and animals, making it increasingly difficult to gather traditional foods and medicines and to access sacred sites and trapline cabins. The day-school and residential-school era promoted the governmental assimilationist policies and punished any expressions of traditional culture, removing Indigenous children from their families, homes, communities, and traditional lifeways.

One House Many Nations and Opaskwayak Cree Nation

The One House Many Nations project at Opaskwayak Cree Nation started in a unique way. Architects from Decentralized Design Lab (DDL), an American architecture and design research lab, became involved with the project following an investigation of Canadian softwood-lumber harvesting practices and conversations with Idle No More co-founder Sylvia McAdam about the destructive clearcutting that was happening on her territory and disrupting her community's land base.[3] Early conversations between Idle No More and DDL were centred around ways in which the wood harvested in the northern boreal forest might be used to build homes, and whether a design for an affordable wood house could be developed, a technology that could productively disrupt the way housing is provided on reserve. On-reserve housing is currently constructed using conventional Western building techniques and processes that force material dependencies on First Nations. First Nation communities would like to separate from these techniques and processes but, to date, most First Nations do not have the capital needed to compete with Western markets.

---

3   See the video *Her Father's Land*, which provides more background on Sylvia's story: https://vimeo.com/78706977

The Hack

Initially, Idle No More asked DDL to design a room and furniture out of wood-pallet material being dumped at the Opaskwayak landfill. Almost immediately, the outfitting of a room transformed into a house constructed of wood panels made from upcycled wood-pallet material that had been nailed and laminated together. This strategy was intended to save costs, but the situation quickly exposed a much more disturbing narrative. What was conceived of as a house in the middle of the boreal forest, made from recycled wood pallets used to ship in material commodities, reflected the economic dependencies on the colonial systems that make, and keep, the people in the community (whom our design was intended to house) homeless.

This concept was never realized. The scale of the housing problem and the volume of material required was too large, and the nuances of supplying and sorting a steady stream of useable pallet material into the production of a housing system were too difficult to take on as a feasible housing solution.

An initial goal of the One House Many Nations campaign was, through community and grassroots support, to produce one house for a community member in need. This small, actionable step could then grow over time to provide more houses. This was the strategy for the house in the Big River One House project, a mini-home that was completed by a small group of people to demonstrate the feasibility of the project concept, which was then communicated through social media and grassroots networks (i.e., "the moccasin telegraph") for others to follow.

The challenge of this kind of project-based approach is the way in which it builds long-term capacity within communities to continue constructing houses once the initial project is built. The one-off project depends on key personnel and, while others contribute meaningfully to the project by donating money, time, labour, and knowledge, it is difficult to translate the particular knowledge gained by the project coordinators, which is context- and community-specific, to those who support – and would potentially be able to replicate – such a project, but are physically removed from it.

These community differences reveal the complexity of the One House Many Nations project. While the struggle for quality affordable housing is universal, the solutions for individual homes in different communities, and even within a community, are unique and require contextual adaptation, community input, and capacity building to maintain. What's more, OCN has approximately 3200 members living on reserve land who are supported by approximately 650 housing units. The band's waiting list for housing is now above 700 units, which, if granted, would more than double the housing infrastructure on the reserve. Combine this with the diversity of individuals', families', and the community's housing needs, and you have a wicked[4] problem with multiple changing, and at times conflicting, requirements. Wicked problems are incredibly messy and complex, difficult to define, have multiple resolutions for multiple conflicted stakeholders, and are hard to evaluate in the near-term.

OCN Design Lab

The design research for the One House Many Nations project looks to shift the definition of high-performance housing away from just technical performance (measurements based on building-scale material, mechanical optimization, and energy efficiency) and toward social performance (measurements based on local material use, community inclusion and capacity building, and the reconnection of people to the land). Performance that is based solely on efficiency of individual buildings is ineffective when trying to optimize for community-scaled performance. When operating within complex adaptive systems, such as a community, one cannot simply assume that, by making an individual process more efficient, the effect on the larger system will be increased efficiency (Ackoff, 1991). In fact, most often when one process is made more efficient in isolation, the net effect on the system, as a whole, is an increased inefficiency (Kay, 2002). Architects who develop solutions without considering the broader ecological and social impact of buildings have created a serious performance problem when looking at buildings in aggregate (i.e., when trying to design for smart-growth dynamic communities).

    The physical design of the house developed through a set of workshops that we termed the OCN Design Lab. On February 17 and 18, 2017, the One House Many Nations team, which consisted of people from Idle No More and DDL, hosted two day-long design workshops in The Pas, Manitoba. The workshops

---

4   See Rittel & Webber (1973) for a discussion of wicked problems as a response to positivistic and limiting theories of planning.

gave future residents agency to help define how this system should work and what should be included in it. Participants also drew and discussed what their ideal house and/or village would look and feel like. The initial design workshop yielded about a dozen community designs that were condensed into four house concepts, which were distilled into the initial OCN One House Many Nations prototype.

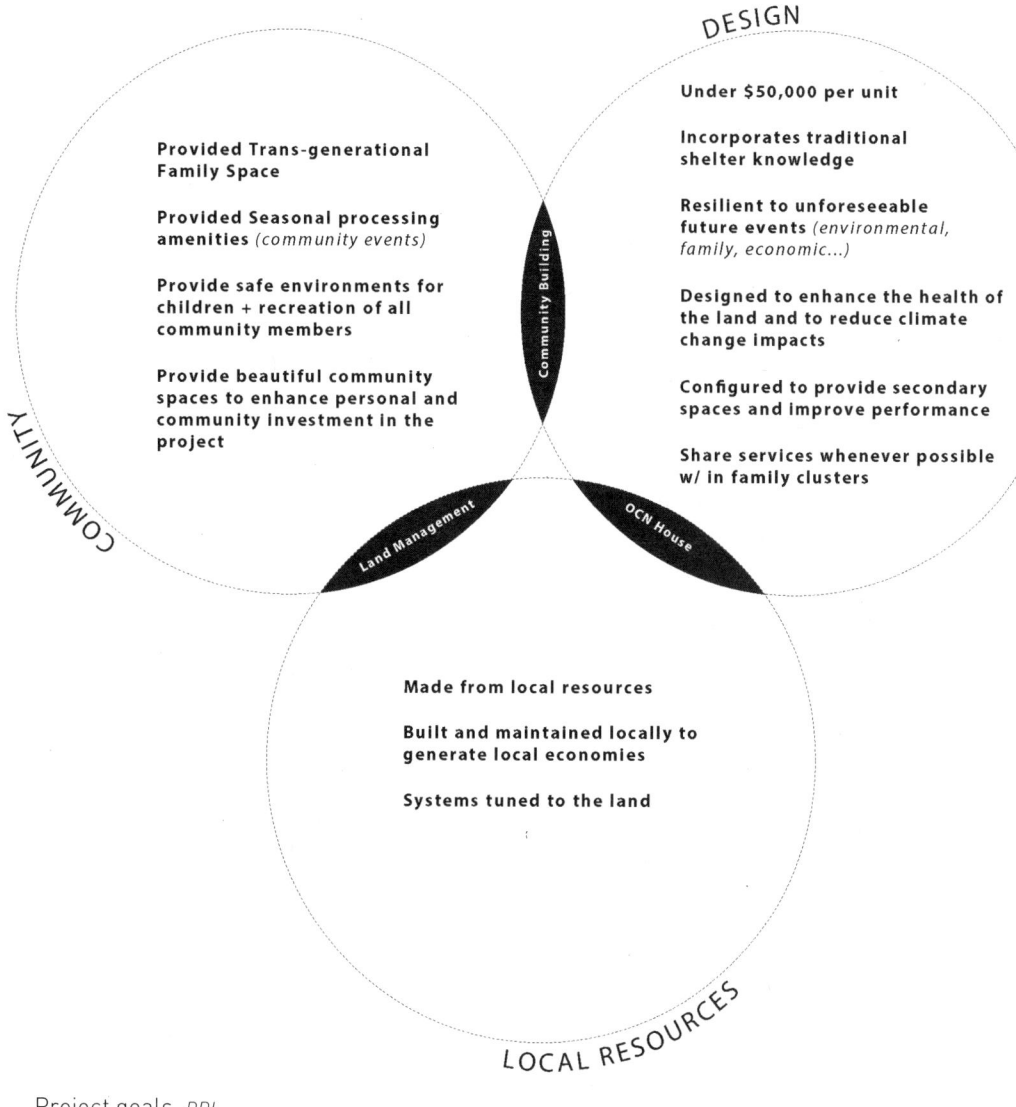

DESIGN

Under $50,000 per unit

Incorporates traditional shelter knowledge

Resilient to unforeseeable future events *(environmental, family, economic...)*

Designed to enhance the health of the land and to reduce climate change impacts

Configured to provide secondary spaces and improve performance

Share services whenever possible w/ in family clusters

COMMUNITY

Provided Trans-generational Family Space

Provided Seasonal processing amenities *(community events)*

Provide safe environments for children + recreation of all community members

Provide beautiful community spaces to enhance personal and community investment in the project

LOCAL RESOURCES

Made from local resources

Built and maintained locally to generate local economies

Systems tuned to the land

Community Building · *Land Management* · *OCN House*

Project goals. *DDL*

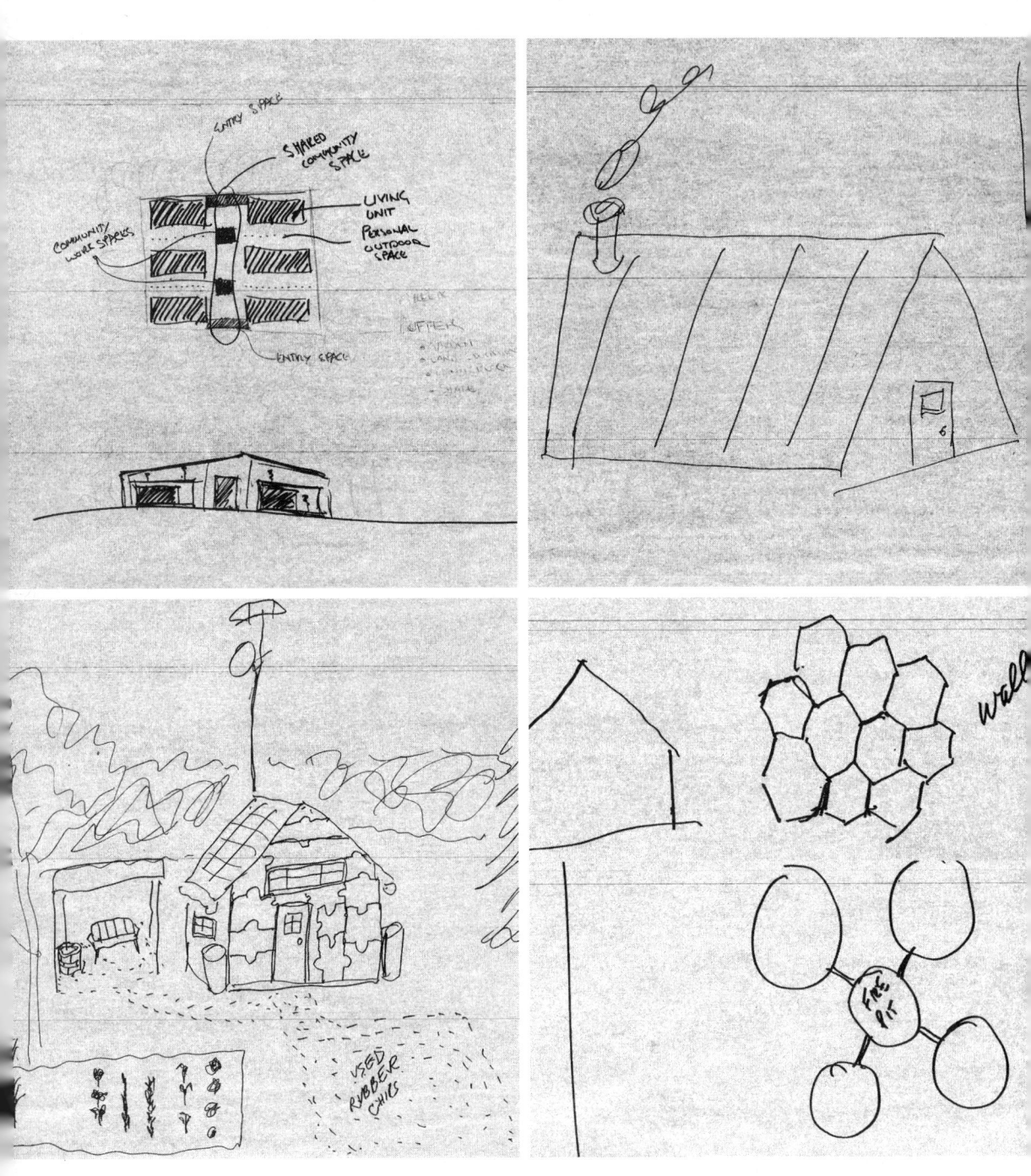

Some community design workshop ideas. *OCN DESIGN LAB*

The team held a community design lab on June 11, 2017, where OCN members and members of the OCN Design Lab used a game model to explore different house and village configurations based on their own personal and family conditions. Based on these tested configurations and budget constraints, an initial prototype design for the house was determined and the design was developed for construction.

Prototype at Expo for Design, Innovation, and Technology (EDIT 2017)

Funding for the initial OCN prototype was supported by the University of Minnesota's Grant-In-Aid program and their Institute for Diversity, Equity, and Advocacy. In addition, cash and in-kind support was provided by the OCN Design Lab, Idle No More, Spruce Products (a local lumber mill), and community members from OCN and The Pas. A prototype was designed that could be assembled in Toronto at the Expo for Design, Innovation, and Technology (EDIT 2017, September 28–October 8, 2017). It was constructed in part in The Pas, Manitoba, and in part in Hinckley, Minnesota, before it was shipped to Toronto. Once there, it was assembled and used to highlight issues relating to the shortage and quality of Indigenous housing across Canada.

Design lab held on June 11, 2017. OCN members configured different utility and living modules to create their own ideal house design and village constellation. *OCN DESIGN LAB*

The prototype consists of two types of units, shelter modules and service modules, which are linked together. This modular design allows the house to be expanded on and/or reconfigured to meet the unique needs of individual homeowners. Modules come in two geometrical types, rectangular and triangular. The triangular modules contain the house's utilities and allow it to rest nimbly on the land, maneuvering delicately through sites with irregular boundaries or around trees and other landscape features. The square units are living and sleeping spaces, constructed out of solid wood panels that act as heat sinks to moderate the house's temperature in the summer and winter. The solid wood panels resist mold and mildew problems because they lack internal cavity spaces where water vapour

Prototype at EDIT 2017. *ONE HOUSE MANY NATIONS*

can condense. The panels used in the prototype were manufactured in the United States, but the team is now working to develop a solid wood panel system that could be produced by the community, using local materials.

This prototype of an individual house was designed to configure into a larger village, the design principles of which were established through the community design workshops. Each unit is designed to plug back into a central community hub that supplies utilities to a cluster of houses that in turn form a village constellation. Distributing systems to the houses in this way reduces overall village costs per house. The central utility hub also serves as a community centre, providing amenity spaces for large-scale gatherings, teaching programs, cooking, and seasonal food processing.

CHAPTER 11   181

OCN Sustainable Village Concept

Following EDIT, the prototype was transported back to OCN territory and reassembled. From the onset of the project at OCN, the design of a house has always been framed within the development of a village. From the initial presentation of the concept to Chief and Council by members from

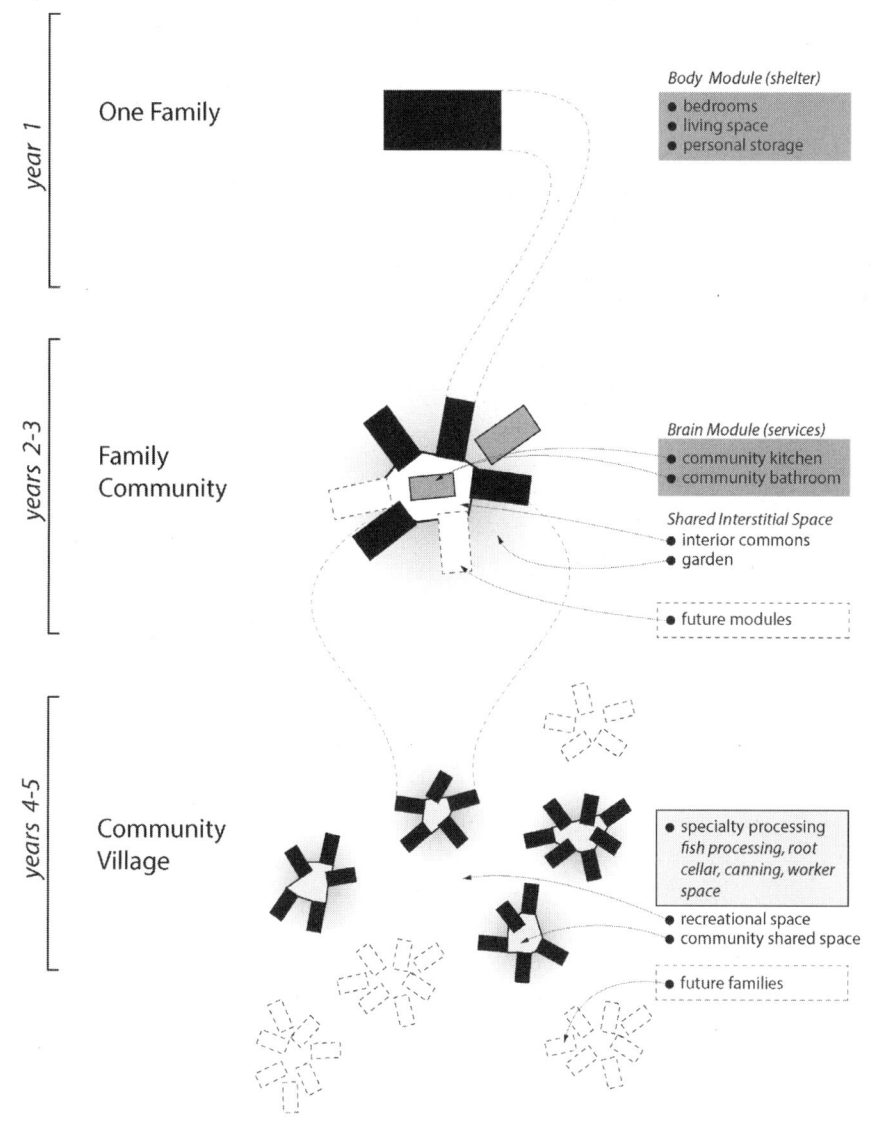

year 1 — One Family

Body Module (shelter)
- bedrooms
- living space
- personal storage

years 2-3 — Family Community

Brain Module (services)
- community kitchen
- community bathroom

Shared Interstitial Space
- interior commons
- garden

- future modules

years 4-5 — Community Village

- specialty processing *fish processing, root cellar, canning, worker space*
- recreational space
- community shared space

- future families

Village progression diagram from Chief and Council presentation, December 2016. *DDL*

Idle No More, DDL, and the community, the design of an individual house was thought of as a component within the larger design of a sustainable village.

How the construction of houses can be used to dismantle colonial models continues to be an evolving question within the project. One example of the way this is done is that the prototype's foundation is made of basic wooden cribbing, with the wooden building volumes above tied back down to the ground with earth anchors. This strategy is being explored because it is less expensive than concrete foundations and also has a lower ecological impact, as there is less site disturbance and lower embodied energy in the system (less energy goes into the manufacturing processing for wood than for concrete). This kind of attachment to the earth is also less permanent, allowing whoever owns the house to take the equity they invest in the house with them should they move, i.e., they can take the modules apart and bring their house with them. Designing locally sourced and locally manufactured building components is another way to make communities less dependent on existing colonial economic systems.

Reflection

One of the most important reflections on the project was the realization that the housing crisis is not a building problem, it is a systems problem. Limited support for education, reduced economic opportunity, insufficient social-support structures, and forced separation from the land and cultural traditions all reduce people's and communities' access to the resources and knowledge needed to source, construct, and maintain housing. There will continue to be a housing shortage as long as the systems remain that make and keep people homeless. The larger opportunity of this project is to hack these systems (education, economics, environmental exploitation) through design strategies that decolonize the sourcing, manufacturing, construction, and training attached to housing. As we transition from the "house" to the "village" prototype, the OCN Design Lab will continue to press against existing colonial systems. Community projects, whatever their physical scope, need an anti-oppression educational component that extends the project to take on the systems that caused it and that inform the decisions made about it. This is the potential of project-based learning – to create lasting change.

Recognizing Indigenous resistance and uplifting resurgence is a necessity for any decolonial project. Indigenous knowledge systems are valid and life-giving.

However, colonial housing models have not only violently reshaped Indigenous social structures, they have constricted the way we think about a building's performance. Many of the challenges we face deal with conforming to provincial codes, which is a requirement for projects that receive Indigenous and Northern Affairs Canada (INAC) funding. Our intention in pushing against codes is not to produce less safe or substandard houses, but to produce houses that adhere to our agenda of dismantling colonial systems. This agenda includes the building code, which we understand helps ensure that housing is safe but, at the same time, restricts construction of housing to designs that may fit well with the needs of people living in urban centres or agricultural regions, but does not always fit the housing needs of First Nations communities. We hope that, ultimately, the code will be revised so that it is capable both of ensuring that First Nations housing is safe and of enabling the construction of housing that First Nations people want to live in. Building performance should not be defined at the building scale; buildings have a relationship with their environment. They are sourced from it and house people whose lives are dependent on it. They are part of the environment, both economic and ecologic. The knowledge gained by designing and constructing your house may have as much long-term value and cost savings as sealing and super-insulating it to reduce energy costs. This project is working to define a building's performance by its socioecological relationship to the land and the communities that it supports.

Collaboration

The One House Many Nations collaborators have made a commitment to maintain a decolonizing agenda throughout this project. This commitment has required us to consistently leverage the differences between settler and Indigenous perspectives and experiences. In the course of executing our physical project, we regularly bump up against the colonial systems (codes, zoning, financial systems, professional expertise, Western education) that we are actually trying to dismantle. One of the challenges of working on wicked problems is that they contain multiple, often shifting, goals – and this project is no exception. Unconventional form, affordability, local manufacturing, mass production, customizable design, land-based education, practical training, shared space-making, home ownership, and modularity/flexibility converge in the One House

Many Nations project, all within a decolonizing design framework that presses against colonial regulations while relying, at times, on funding streams that require some level of colonial compliance.

Within a project as complex as One House Many Nations, relationships are critical, particularly when non-Indigenous people are working in First Nations communities. One House Many Nations is an Indigenous-led initiative that reached out to DDL to invite their participation and collaboration in the OCN project. Over the course of the project, the cohesiveness of the project team was challenged, at times, by the differences between our cultures, values, and communication styles, our positions in the colonial history of the Americas, and the ways in which that history has constructed our present-day relationships to privilege and power. In these moments, those invited into the community to share in the work have been able to reflect on their role (and, in some instances, complicity) in the systems that the work is trying to dismantle. Resolving these challenges has sometimes helped to strengthen relationships and led to clearer or more refined understandings of the project as a whole. At other times, these challenges have irreparably damaged working relationships; collaborators have left the project and new relationships had to be formed to continue the work. The forced typological change and regulation of housing in Indigenous communities has been an act of colonial violence, and the work done in the One House Many Nations to address it is one part of a complex and contested long-term project.

References

Ackoff, R. (1991). Continuous Improvement-I. *Systems Practice, 4*(5), 393-95.

Assembly of First Nations. (June 2013). *Fact sheet: First Nations housing on-reserve*. Retrieved from https://www.afn.ca/uploads/files/housing/factsheet-housing.pdf

Cannon, M. (1998). The regulation of First Nations sexuality. *The Canadian Journal of Native Studies, 18*(1), 1-18.

Gauthier, S., Bernier, P., Kuuluvainen, T., Shvidenko, D., & Schepaschenko, G. (2015). Boreal forest health and global change. *Science, 349*, 819-822. doi: 10.1126/science.aaa9092

Gilio-Whitaker, D. (2015). Idle No More and fourth world social movements in the new millennium. *South Atlantic Quarterly, 114*(4), 866-877. doi:10.1215/00382876-3157391

Hyslop, K. (2017, March 24). Margolese prize winner wants homelessness no more. *The Tyee*. Retrieved from https://thetyee.ca/News/2017/03/24/Sylvia-McAdam-Interview/

Idle No More. (2015, October 07). *Idle No More launches the One House, Many Nations campaign*. Retrieved from http://www.idlenomore.ca/idle_no_more_launches_the_one_house_many_nations_campaign

Jacobs, J. (1985). *Cities and the wealth of nations.* New York, NY: Vintage Books.

Kay, J. J. (2002). On complexity theory, exergy, and industrial ecology. In C. Kibert, J. Sendzimir, & G. Guy (Eds.), *Construction ecology: Nature as the basis for green buildings.* New York, NY: Spon Press.

McLean, S. (2014). Restorying Canada. In Kino-nda-niimi Collective (Ed.), *The winter we danced: Voices from the past, the future, and the Idle No More movement.* Winnipeg, MB: ARP Books.

Perry, A. (2003). From "the hot-bed of vice" to the "good and well-ordered Christian home": First Nations housing and reform in nineteenth-century British Columbia. *Ethnohistory, 50*(4), 587-610. doi: https://doi.org/10.1215/00141801-50-4-587

Rittel, H., & Webber, W. (1972). Dilemmas in a general theory of planning. *Policy Sciences, 4*(2), 155-169.

Smith, W., & Cheng, R. (2015). *Canada's intact forest landscapes.* Ottawa, ON: Global Forest Watch Canada.

Wilson, A. (2015). A steadily beating heart: Indigenous resistance and resurgence. In E. Coburn (Ed.), *More will sing their way to freedom: Indigenous resistance and resurgence.* Winnipeg, MB: Fernwood.

Wilson, A., & Pilar, P. (2018, January 16). Grounding the currents of Indigenous resistance. *Roar Magazine.* Retrieved from https://roarmag.org/essays/indigenous-peoples-resistance-americas/

Woolsey, C. (2013). The Indian Act: The social engineering of Canada's First Nations. *Explorations in Anthropology, 12*(1), 20-30.

Woons, Marc. (2013, November 2). The "Idle No More" movement and global indifference to Indigenous nationalism [online]. *AlterNative: An International Journal of Indigenous Peoples, 9*(2), 172-177.

About the Author
Bonnie Ferguson-Baird is a wife, and mother of three. Her background in social work, education, and intentional parenting has led her down a path (surprisingly) toward homeschooling. With the eldest in university, one near graduation, and a creative 12-year-old bringing up the rear, her reflections about what, how, and when we learn, and how we address group work and project-based learning, come from a unique perspective.

Who Should Read This Chapter?
Anyone interested in a natural approach to learning.

The Theme of This Chapter in Three Words
Readiness brings growth.

As an Educator, What Are You Passionate About?
As an educator, I am passionate first and foremost about people growing into who they are intended to be. I believe that growth will happen naturally if we offer opportunities and remove barriers (if possible) that distract and cloud learning. Those aspects of life we can't control become part of the learning journey and add to the development of who we are. Nurturing our ability to connect, serve, love, learn, communicate, find compassion, solve problems, challenge, and express ourselves comes alongside academic training to create a complete experience of learning and growing that lasts a lifetime.

CHAPTER 12

Home-School Projects: Are They Learning the Right Stuff?

Bonnie Ferguson-Baird
Winnipeg, Manitoba, Canada

We home-school. As a home-learning family, many questions arise, but one big one continues to surface. We ask it of ourselves, and others ask it of us. Can anyone possibly be learning anything? Are our kids learning the right stuff? Can projects teach us the right stuff?

For many of us home-learners, project-based learning and home-schooling go hand in hand. Life is a project. It's a compilation of experiences, opportunities, risks, failures, and successes that build on one another and create a journey. It's almost impossible to pick apart and identify the individual moments of learning that lead to that beautiful place of competency and confidence.

We all want to be sure we can answer these questions confidently, but what if these are not the right questions to ask?

Learning the right stuff implies that someone knows what knowledge needs to be offered and when. It's as if we saturate sponges with specific skills and then offer them to the students so that they can squeeze out the same information when we request it. But how fascinating to consider that what the sponge is saturated with produces something different for each individual when they squeeze it. The stuff that goes into the sponge produces two things when squeezed – something predictable and something unpredictable, something anticipated and yet also completely unique, depending on the needs, dreams, experiences, and abilities of the learner. All home-schooling parents have fears, but we are also confident in one simple truth – we learn. Always. But we learn in our own time. We learn *what* we need to *when* we need to.

Passion breeds learning. When working with our home-schooling family, we try to access those passions through project-based learning. For us, this means engaging with a process through a framework that makes room for learning both the planned and the unplanned. It's about recognizing the value in the process itself and acknowledging that learning is unique. Project-based learning allows for learning things that we have no control over. We can provide a framework for what we want to learn, and we can decide what knowledge to offer, but how it gets absorbed and squeezed out of the sponge is beyond our control. To try to control the learning process would limit the depth and breadth of what we're uniquely designed to learn. We need to trust that kids want to learn. Education isn't something you get; it's something you grow, and we are designed to grow. When we as educators try to control what is learned, the learner loses their control. This loss of control deflates passion. And if we can't help someone find their own passion, we leave them with nothing in the end. They leave this journey of education with nothing of their own – just a compilation of other people's passions and expectations.

So, are they learning the right stuff? Are we teaching the right stuff? I'm not sure these questions should be our focus. The questions instead might be: "Are we offering the right opportunities?" "Can we offer the guidance they need?" "Have I built a strong enough relationship with these unique individuals so that I can offer guidance and they will welcome it?" We are designed to learn. Learning can't be helped when we are excited or interested or even disgusted. It is not a process done to us; it is a process of natural flow. That is, unless we dam it, and then wonder why it has stopped flowing. Our job is to present numerous sponges, saturated with different skills and opportunities, and to build relationship so there is a safe place to learn. Yes, we may need to clarify the framework. We may need to hand someone the sponge, or lay sponges out and see what is picked up. We may need to clearly define how the process could work, and come alongside until they are comfortable handling the sponge themselves. Or we may need to step back and watch. These actions are all required of us at different times and will become clear through each relationship, but we're still not in control of what is released from the sponge, nor should we want to be. We need to get out of the way as they start to squeeze. We won't be carrying those sponges for them into adulthood, so it is our role to help them understand the lifelong intricacies of the process of learning. Then, as more opportunities come up throughout their lives, they will be equipped to squeeze. Project-based learning sets the stage for learning – a place to pick up your sponges and begin the journey of seeing what you can squeeze out that nourishes you, both as a person and as an individual.

These questions about learning the right stuff arise when we don't have a clear idea of what is actually required of us as individuals and communities in order to feel fulfilled and be contributing members of society. What is our dream, individually and collectively; what do we *really* need to know? I need to know how to resolve conflict, how to say sorry, and how to fix a problem I created. I need to know how to support someone else who messed up, rather than lay blame. Yes, I also need academics, and I need to exercise my brain, my strengths, and my gifts, along with challenging myself to discover new things. I need to overcome fear, to take risks, to want to continue to learn past my school years. Project-based learning allows for a richer, more complete layering of learning to better equip students to grow into strong, confident, adaptable people who can get along with others.

Patience.

Patience.

Patience.

An educational career is a long one – kindergarten to grade 12 and beyond. Therefore, we have a treasured gift; the gift of time. Sponges can't sit in individual age boxes or a box with a year stamped on them; they will dry out. There is a fluidity to project-based learning that allows us to carry our sponges with us through time. That is the constant challenge for us to remember as we and others ask these questions.

When I started home-schooling, I panicked each spring. Have we covered enough? Did anybody learn anything? How many things can I squeeze in before June is over? And, more poignantly, why do they have to happen before June is over? As the years go by, I too carry my sponges, and continue to pour information into them and watch what comes out. I've learned that learning happens. Our kids *are* learning things, many of which I didn't list on my outline of studies for the year. They're not necessarily the things I saturated the sponges with, but our kids definitely managed to squeeze something beautiful out of what was put in. Learning happens, but often not as I envisioned. Instead, it happens according to the unique desires, learning styles, needs, and life opportunities of each of our three very different children. And I haven't been able to delineate exactly what school year they learned them in. Often my government reports state that we are "continuing to work on" or "I see growth in" or "I'm excited that I'm beginning to see." I've come to know that, by the end of grade 12, many things will have been learned, and I won't be completely sure when or how they happened. I will have provided the framework, and I can tell you when the framework was offered, but exactly when multiplication was understood at a deep level, I definitely couldn't pinpoint. It's clear, though, that the freedom to grow through time, without yearly boundaries, has led to a natural individualized growth. A growth that sticks, becomes part of your reality, and does not fall away after exams. Project-based learning can support this kind of growth.

We've educated two of our children through high school (which was definitely not in our original plan). Our oldest is now in university, studying math and physics, and our daughter is in grade 12, an avid lover of history and geography, taking a few courses at the University of Winnipeg Collegiate. The 12-year-old is juggling many sponges at the moment, trying to complete seatwork expectations but, more enjoyably, using a hot glue gun to join cardboard and metal scraps or dressing up like a Viking. We're enjoying the process, and we've come to relax about it. We've learned alongside many other home-schooling families and have walked a journey with many of these children into adulthood. I share this to say that I've seen the results. We're no longer in the throes of early years, when project-based learning is somewhat natural. Project-based learning throughout the entire school career allows space and time for development over the years and brings layers of maturity to the surface. These young adults have gone off to university, often specialized universities, community college, or full-time jobs. They know themselves, or at least know how to discover themselves as they continue to grow. They contribute. They can relate to people of different ages, including adults and young children. Learning over a span of years, rather than compartmentalizing learning into segregated sections, means that we have the opportunity to offer more sponges, to direct our kids toward sponges that lead into the next stage we see developing (or not developing) in a person's life. The more sponges available to squeeze, the more that can be released. When we look at the journey of learning over the long term, we can see the flow and offer sponges to fill in the cracks as we see them forming. We can offer alternative options or experiences that can augment or enhance what is being learned. We can see the learning process more comprehensively.

Do we need to be told what to do? Absolutely. Often. If you have kids, you know that sometimes you just want them to do what they're told. But there are many things we do not need to be told to do – to breathe, to think, or to learn. I can offer information, encouragement, direction, yes, but I can't make them learn. That is a process that happens within each person, for many different reasons. Have you ever taught a child something, say 50 times, to have them forget it repeatedly, and then come to share with you an amazing insight they learned from some other random encounter? The very same insight you offered over and over again? Why is that? Readiness, for one thing. It's something we cannot produce for them. Something happens within us that opens a door when we're ready to be receptive – developmental readiness, academic readiness, emotional readiness, and the list goes on. The factors that contribute to our readiness are endless and, as a social worker, I know that adverse childhood reactions have everything to do with the readiness to learn. To learn math, and to learn to be with others. To learn science, and to learn how to look someone in the eye. To learn history, and to learn to say what needs to be said. You get the point.

Readiness is clearly connected to our emotional bank accounts. When they're filled, we can see and feel the openness, the readiness, to learn. When our basic needs are not met – we're hungry, angry, or have a break in a relationship that needs to be reconnected – learning stops. I can actually see it happening. Someone says something that hurts your heart, opens an old relational wound, or throws a book and hits you, and your ability to learn in that moment evaporates instantly. Without addressing these things as part of the process, you lose the opportunity of seeing what really needs to be learned – how to reconnect after a break in a relationship, how to say you're sorry for throwing a book, or how to express how you feel to someone you love. These skills are absolutely as important as any academic learning and are carried into every part of adult life. Not having the chance to practise them when the moment arises is a disservice to our learning process and to our children as growing individuals. Process, the action involved in moving forward toward some end, is as important as the end itself. The outcome is useless without the process. Project-based learning enables readiness through this use of process, because you can be ready in a multitude of areas and not ready in others, and yet you can learn as much as you're ready to learn through a process that is limitless in opportunities.

We are part of a home-school collective. Eight families meet one afternoon a week to share learning, community, and relationship. Our children range in age from 4 to 17, and we learn and teach together. There is nothing particularly special about us; we're just passionate and intentional about our families and the learning and community we can create. Learning together brings more opportunities than we can obtain on our own. In 2008, we decided to embark on a new journey and took on a project. We would stage a Shakespeare play, and have it be as professional as we could make it. We could sense the rich layers of learning that such a project could offer: learning about Shakespeare, memorizing, text work, sewing costumes, building props, selling tickets, teamwork. A few of us had some experience in directing, sewing, and building. Surely, if we pulled together, something beautiful could happen. Well, something beautiful did happen, in the end, although it might have looked awful to the naked eye.

The final outcome, of course, was one very small part of what was produced.

The learning outcomes were clear. We, as parents, could begin to saturate the sponges by offering guidance, direction, and teaching in areas like sewing, building, memorizing, line-work, history, blocking, drama games, etc. This process began just after Christmas, during our weekly afternoon together. The process was slow. Very few of us knew what this would actually look like in the end, but we continued to saturate, hoping that when the kids started squeezing we would see where this was going.

Well, there was very little squeezing going on, and lots of saturating. In fact, the parents were working hard. So far, lots of input was producing very little output. We would ask who was interested in building and design, and many kids would come to talk about how the set could look, offering huge extravagant dreams that needed to be brought back to reality. We had limited time (one afternoon a week), experience, and no budget. Slowly, interested designers would drift off as the hands-on work needed to be done, sliding into a group that they were more interested in. But as the show dates loomed closer and closer, the energy from the kids started to change. They needed each other. The main work they needed to do was to memorize and act. It became our job to fill in those holes so they could focus on the acting. Suddenly, subtle questions started to arise. If I forget my lines, how will I be prompted to remember my line? If someone else stands in the wrong place, where will I stand? How will I fix it without embarrassing us both in front of an audience? What will I do if I forget my prop? What will I do if someone else forgets their prop? Is responding in anger going to fix this mess, or would encouragement do better after someone messes up a line in front of the whole world? We're all vulnerable here, but not just individually – as a community too. How will we handle our vulnerability? Do we know how? Can we do what we want to under pressure? What if we can't? Will these friendships hold? Or, do I really want to do this? If I don't, do I need to carry on for the sake of the troupe? What exactly does commitment mean?

These questions are big and, of course, there are more. They're bigger than a play; they're more important to becoming a strong, compassionate, adaptable adult than pulling off Shakespeare.

Once a week became twice a week around the beginning of March. Suddenly, we were all working hard, together. The original framework had been laid out, and we were squeezing learning out everywhere. We had a theatre, costumes, props, direction. We had a play. We were rehearsing every day now for two weeks of tech as we put the finishing touches on our costumes, our lines, our props, our blocking.

And then, it's play week, the most magical week of the entire year. The air feels different. The energy is electric. The relationships are intense, real, necessary. We feel a deep emotion that is hard to identify. All of a sudden, what is dripping from this beautiful mess is a nectar like none other. We begin to see in practical form what has been absorbed through this process and is now being squeezed out, in addition to the original learning outcomes. Someone picks up a dropped prop as they make their stage exit; a 10-year-old skips some lines on purpose because a co-actor forgot to bring the prop on stage for them to refer to; the whole troupe searches for cough drops to soothe a friend, and then, watching from the wings, they hold their breath, waiting to see if she can deliver her lines without giving way to a coughing fit. Someone else is holding their friend backstage because they're discouraged after messing up a scene, and 16-year-olds are playing games with 7-year-olds to help calm their nerves while they wait to go onstage. Others are working hard to respect the privacy of the introvert who's trying to carve out some space and stay focused in a noisy, crowded greenroom, provided everyone is not frantically searching for a missing boot for the actor on stage in his white sport socks. Gratitude flows with tears, and many are approaching others with encouraging words after they've messed up and feel they just can't go on stage again. Backstage chants are sung to solidify solidarity; notes are given to each individual outlining specific ways they've grown and nurtured the troupe. Children are finding each parent, and thanking them for their work, love, and support. These may sound like simple things, but they're things that build character; they add to the richness of the learning – both the seen and the unseen – that is available when we embark on a project together.

Many of the things we learned throughout this lengthy project were not developed in the first year. We were new to this. We were still very raw.

As the years went by, however, new sponges were added. They became obvious; they presented themselves. This project progressed over time and left room for flexibility for all of us to grow, to add to the framework and strengthen it, letting additional experiences strengthen the process. We added to the project early on, adding original text rather than adopting an adapted version. Time allowed us to fine-tune the project.

That first year lit a fire that would last a decade. In fact, a Fringe Festival troupe is a direct offshoot of this project. These Knavish Hedgehogs have consistently won four- and five-star reviews over the years. When we started, though, a few of these young people were content to be stagehands. They were too afraid to trust themselves in front of an audience. It was simply too much of a stretch beyond their comfort zone. Over time, they ventured well beyond knowing when to move set pieces without being seen. They learned how to let their peers shine publicly. They learned how to embrace their own gifts, and they learned how to challenge themselves to ask the hard questions. Is anything holding me back from trying something new and scary? Am I able to try something new, and go further than I ever thought I could?

Time and space that we allocated to let these questions flow, and then develop, paid off. Some of those kids have since appeared on the Manitoba Theatre Centre Mainstage. Not because they started as great actors, but because they learned something about themselves beyond the acting – something we couldn't anticipate or plan for. It was unique and necessary for who they were to become and their own tender journey, supported and scaffolded by a framework, but designed and authored by themselves. This discovery is not something that could have been anticipated or foreseen. Space had to be made for the personal process to unfold. It didn't happen within one school year. It happened over many years of freedom to try new things, to fail, grow, develop, change, and succeed.

But fail we did. Many times. In fact, the moms hired a mediator to help us work through the intensity of emotion that surfaced as so many people worked together so closely.

Failure? An inadequate word, really.

We found new things to learn about ourselves, others, our friendships, our community. We learned what matters. We learned what doesn't. What a gift for our kids to learn – how to graciously and directly tackle hurt feelings, to see their teachers, leaders, parents, and mentors working through emotions and coming out stronger as individuals and as a community. No failure here. Failure is a gift – not failure to complete a particular project, but the guaranteed failure that will accompany any project. This is where real learning happens.

Struggles? Yes, there were many. But after nine years, these kids have found things to love that they might not have experienced without a solid framework to springboard from. Not all of these kids (in fact, very few) have developed an interest in professional acting. But they've found something in themselves because of what was offered to them – an opportunity offered within a strong framework. Sure, there was lots of room for personal development and growth, but the framework offered stability and room for confidence to emerge within a safe environment. Who knew one could fall in love with Shakespeare, feel proud of knowing how to pull apart and understand English from around four hundred years ago, memorize hundreds of lines, or make a costume? Discovering new things about ourselves builds a confidence we can carry with us to other challenges and opportunities that will come our way.

We've equipped our kids with more than a bit of Shakespeare. They've squeezed out a confidence, an ability to venture into the unknown with hope, an adaptability to handling life when it changes before their eyes. To know that we don't have to be the best; we only have to be *our* best. To know that we are able, supported, unique. We are capable of dreaming and creating our life, though it may get messy, and we may need a mediator. In fact, it *will* get messy. Life will take turns we weren't expecting. But projects such as this one can help us know that adapting is actually part of the journey – it is not an accident that needs fixing. It is predictable in its unpredictability, and part of the process of life. And we can get through it. We can even embrace it with joy.

Project-based learning, by its very nature, will look different every time. Different teachers and mentors, with different students, in different environments, all lead to different learning experiences. For our learning cooperative, project-based learning looked like this: we started with an idea, and we shared it with the group. The adults did some research and discussion in order to present something that the kids could hang on to, something they could understand. We brainstormed together, and we created a vision together.

This began a creative process that allowed us all to access thoughts that had not yet come to the surface. It was a process of finding those questions, those ideas, and putting them out to the group so they could be sifted and refined. A framework started to take shape. We discovered what it meant to be vulnerable with each other, to be brave enough to share what others might not agree with or appreciate. Also, to hear the ideas of others without judgment. Then, to let those ideas ferment and see what could realistically be agreed upon by the group. We discussed which ideas were manageable enough to consider, and which ideas could be reshaped to bring their essence to life if they couldn't happen in their entirety. We had the opportunity to manage the feelings that surfaced when our idea was not chosen, and learned to be okay with it because we were committed to the group. We needed to learn that our opinion mattered. We needed to feel heard individually, even if we agreed as a group to take a different path than what someone had hoped for on a personal level. We learned to compromise. We learned to adapt, and to offer creative suggestions toward a collective goal. We learned to express ourselves. We learned to speak up, and we learned how and when to be quiet. We learned how to decide what matters, and what doesn't.

We brainstormed exactly what needed to be accomplished for us to complete this task. We decided if we had enough people power to pull it off. We expressed our personal interests, and agreed to help in certain areas. We did the research, and we put in the time to complete the tasks we agreed to. We learned to ask for support, to check in with one another. We encouraged. We had check-in meetings. We had troubleshooting meetings whenever feelings had been hurt, or whenever we were off-track and needed to realign. How did we do this? We expressed our feelings. We cried. We let things go. We picked things up. We encouraged again and again. This process was by no means perfect, and these tough relational issues were not all wrapped up neatly. But we had the opportunity to start to formulate how we wanted to interact with one another, and to practise responding to people we cared about while remaining true to ourselves.

A project like this also allows for an end date. The show would happen on the dates we'd rented the theatre for, regardless of how ready we felt. We had paid the money – lots of it. And we learned things, lots of things. Although the play had an end date, it was our job to make sure we made time for the other learning that surfaced. This kind of rich learning takes time and patience. It takes processing and discussion. For some, processing is quick and simple, and for others it takes hours of self-reflection, nurturing, and thought. Time for this can be and needs to be factored into project-based learning, along with having the mentorship available to nurture the process.

When we look back, we can see not only the intentional learning outcomes outlined in a framework, but the hidden treasures as well. We learned what we're capable of, and what we're not. We learned how to share our feelings, and how to listen to the feelings of others. We learned to decide if our feelings were more important than those of others, or if we could temper our different feelings and still be friends. We learned how to speak publicly without a script when we went to schools and talked with students to prepare them for the show. We also learned how not to embarrass each other when we were nervous. We learned this, though, because a framework had been put in place. The framework definitely outlined how to memorize lines and build a set piece, but also how to manage our feelings. We discussed these things in advance. We prepared our minds for what could come, and encouraged kids to think about how they might respond, and how they might challenge themselves to respond, rather than reverting to negative responses. How did we challenge ourselves to be better? We set a framework, let each person find what they needed within it, and presented the opportunities to practise. What one person needed to learn was something that came naturally for another – no outcome could possibly be the same.

This process of creating a framework provides safety. It provides a footing to give us our bearings, to stabilize ourselves before the new challenges begin. Project-based learning is not about throwing sponges at each other – it is about carefully listening to who someone is, and choosing sponges that will potentially nurture and fill that person. Although each sponge is squeezed and unique learning comes out, there are some skills the framework accounts for. If you memorize lines and stand in front of an audience, you will learn those particular skills. You will also learn the unique set of skills and character challenges that you're ready to learn at that point in your life. The project framework needs to provide this sense of stability so that the unique learning can also emerge.

We also needed to examine the framework itself and anticipate what could be learned by our family. Our kids are not exceptional actors. None of them wants to be professional actors (except maybe the 12-year-old who thinks it might be a good idea). But the framework of a play enabled them to engage with learning that could provide many different potential learning outcomes that would benefit them, in addition to many outcomes that couldn't be anticipated. Confidence was an area in which we could improve, as well as memorization and English academic content. Challenging yourself outside of your comfort zone and meeting deadlines are vital to the learning process.

There are, of course, many different frameworks that can provide these learning opportunities. We also found many skills lying just under the surface that had a chance to be strengthened – such as easily adapting to change, letting go if something was particularly important to someone else, and sewing one's own costume with a pattern – and this play framework definitely offered a chance to improve these skills. We can learn many things in many different ways. The project – in this case, the play – was just an outlet, a structured, layered project with a start date and end date that lent itself to a certain arena of learning outcomes. The journey we take with any project enables us to learn what we need to when we need to, as well as squeezing out the learning from the basic framework itself.

Learning is for all of us. In our case, we were a group of mothers who worked alongside our children to create a project together. For each of our children, something different was required. Sometimes it was a student who took the reins and designed a poster because they had an interest in doing so. The support required was to help the student to assemble a team and work through how to incorporate the opinions of others. Sometimes it was a parent who took the lead to accomplish a task because the students were focused on other aspects of the play. Other times, graduates would come back to co-direct, do fight choreography, design costumes, or do photography, and they were welcomed into mentorship roles. The idea is that a team is made up of many different people, with various levels of skill or developing skill, and as teachers we have the opportunity to enter into the learning process with our students through a relational experience. We can be there to notice when mentorship is needed or when someone can be challenged to step into leadership, or when some guidance or encouragement needs to be given. Learning from one another brings equality to the process, a deeper understanding that learning is not just for students but is actually for all of us. It gives us all the freedom to learn and to teach. I would dare say that the parents learned as much as any of the kids, and for that opportunity I'm forever grateful. We learned when to step in and when to step back, when to talk and when to listen, when to teach and when to learn. This in itself gave freedom to our kids to know that this process, this journey of learning, is for everyone, and there is enjoyment, safety, and support in doing it together. This is how community is born.

This Shakespeare troupe is just one example of project-based learning. Our family built a house ourselves, created a small sewing business that didn't get far off the ground, followed requests for history clubs, created elaborate costumes late into the night, and shared life with international students. All of these experiences can be viewed as project-based learning – some went well, some not so well, but learning happened. They reflect a layered journey that doesn't just mimic, but embodies, life. Things grow, and things die. A friend once said to me, "Life is long." What an interesting perspective; we do, usually, have lots of time to nurture, water, and squeeze, and then pick up the next sponge, while learning how to put others down. We need to just open up the boundaries of learning through time and let it unfold. In this way, we learn how to experience life to the fullest. What we learn about ourselves and our world can blossom through project-based learning, and this is certainly as important, perhaps even more so, than curricular outcomes. Project-based learning opens up the freedom, the time, and the space to learn, based on what each unique individual needs. Our job is just to keep saturating those sponges of learning, and let them squeeze. Then step back and ask the question again – are they learning the right stuff? With guidance, love, mentorship, rich opportunities, and the space and freedom to grow, how can they not?

CONCLUSION
Assessment for Continuity

Bonnie and Tom, Authors of Chapter 2

Learners are constantly growing, changing how they interact, behave, make decisions, and perform. This multidimensional improvement is what we validate when we assess. We strive to assist the learner in processing – recognizing, understanding, owning, evaluating, and future planning – their socioemotional and intellectual development.

In our experiences, the learner must be at the centre of assessment, directly involved in each step of the process. Before starting a project, the learner works with their advisor to identify their current academic and socio-emotional positionality. The learner and educator build a rubric, identifying criteria and levels specific to the learner and the project. This individualized rubric enables us to compare the learner's progress with himself or herself rather than comparing them with others. The learner works with their advisor to select a project-appropriate group of assessors: the learner, their advisor, another educator, a friend, and at least one other peer. Upon completion, the assessment group meets to reflect on the learner's performance as a student and as a person. They identify how the learner is different now than when they started the project and how this project compares to their previous work. The learner reflects on whether these changes are positive and whether or not they want to see themselves change more in that way or in a different direction.

This type of system encourages learners to process their own development. By focusing on the individual's progress rather than averages, it empowers students to push themselves in ways that are unique and positive for them. In doing this, it promotes reflection, fosters healthy feedback practices, encourages internal motivation, and provides an avenue for real external validation.

Glenys, Author of Chapter 4

The word *assess* has its roots in the Latin word *assidere*: to sit alongside. Assessment in expeditionary learning is guided by the belief that with the learner we can build a picture of their unique knowledge, understandings, strengths and challenges. Assessment is dynamic. It is focused on student growth and includes a broad collection of measures and opportunities. The information that is gathered through assessment shapes the next learning experience.

Learning stories are key elements of assessment. A learning story is a retelling of how a learner has made sense of the world and his or her experience of problem solving (Egan, 1998). Learning stories are a type of personalized, event-specific journal. They are developed with photos, sketches, work samples, and personal comments that provide a firsthand illustration of the learner's experience. Photos taken during the experience attempt to capture moments of learning, struggle, persistence, and success. Because the stories are a retelling of learning experiences, rich in context, they balance knowledge and skills with conceptual understanding and transferability.

Reviewing a learning story offers key insights for planning and for targeted mini-lessons. Cross-referencing the stories with curriculums creates a space for the specific outcomes met by the student to be noted and new goals set.

Learning stories belong to the student; no two stories are the same. Most importantly, these stories are a visual reminder of our commitment to the learning community. No one has gone about their fieldwork, mini-lessons, and workshops alone. All learners have contributed to the shared knowledge of the group, just as all have enjoyed personal successes. A learning story offers a deeper understanding of the lived experience.

Will, Author of Chapter 10

Assessment is not uniform. Assessment needs to be tailored to the subject and learner and responsive to the needs and goals of the class. For assessment of competency regarding the environment, I look to Daniel Goleman, who developed the term *ecoliteracy* as a way to encapsulate the practices of a socially and emotionally engaged person. Goleman outlined five traits to look for: developing empathy for all forms of life; embracing sustainability as a community practice; making the invisible visible; anticipating unintended consequences; and understanding how nature sustains life (Goleman, 2012, p. 133).

Further, Goleman states that working on these practices cultivates "the knowledge, empathy, and action required for practicing sustainable living" (p. 2). When assessing my learners, I'm looking for evidence of growth in these five facets of ecoliteracy in three areas: their attitudes, knowledge, and actions. Learners often arrive at different levels with different entry points. In my view, a curriculum outcome is not necessarily the best tool to assess their attitude, knowledge, and actions. Rather, evidence of growth is based on previously demonstrated evidence, with the aim of an upward or increasing trajectory – more connections made, a greater awareness of one's place on this planet. Students in my classroom are provided with a variety of ways to demonstrate their attitudes, knowledge, and actions around the five facets of ecoliteracy – for example, via projects, field experiences, or reflections. Evidence can be provided in a variety of mediums, such as text, art, or film, or verbally via a biannual exhibition of learning.

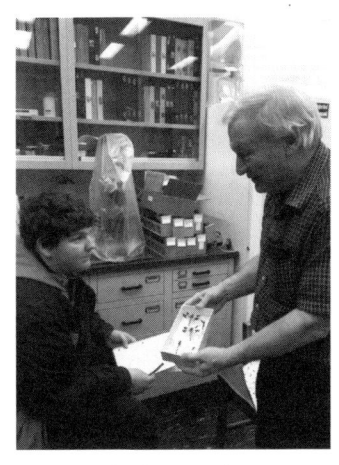

Maples Met learner in dialogue with mentor.

Bonnie, Author of Chapter 12

Assessment takes many forms. In the context of the Shakespeare play, there are some obvious questions to ask. How many people came to each of the four shows? Did they enjoy it? Where did they hear of it? Had they been to previous plays, and would they come again? All these are questions we ask each other, people in the community, family, and so on. and assess before we plan for the next year. But the most meaningful assessment is how we reflect back to one another how we were affected.

Assessment for us looks very much like a celebration – celebrating that whether our project went well or poorly, we succeeded. We stepped up to the challenge, we completed our task, we shared with each other what went well, and we talked about how to make it better. It doesn't look very official, but it has impact just the same.

After everything has been taken down and packed up, we all gather for the cast party. This is the main way we assess. The specifics here are pretty basic, but deeply meaningful. We celebrate not only because we feel we have accomplished something fantastic, but because we need to celebrate each other, and sit in the beauty of the afterglow. We eat, laugh, share stories again and again, and speak out loud the impact of what just happened. We sit in a circle and share one at a time with one another about our favourite moments, what we learned, and how it felt. This is assessment in a sense, but broader; it is that personal moment when you reflect not only on how you contributed, but share how others contributed to you, and how we contributed to each other. We all feel the need to speak it aloud, together. Why we spent all that time and energy becomes exceptionally clear. What we learned is voiced, and this process prepares the way for future challenges. It also acts as another opportunity to strengthen relationships and practise communication skills. This "assessment celebration" assures us that what we all embarked on was worth it and is worth doing again, in whatever form the project happens to take.

Laura, Author of Chapter 5

Assessment within the CIDA-funded Central American community-based agro-conservation project occurred in an ongoing manner and focused on different aspects of the project, depending on project goals, timing within the life of the project, and participants' needs. For providing constructive feedback on the CIDA project as a whole, mid-term and final project reports were helpful to identify successes and challenges. Rural participants and the environment itself provided feedback to university collaborators in a variety of ways: the authenticity of the project, whether interventions were responding to participants' needs, and whether the interventions were worth adopting. At a farm level, nature gave feedback on the efficacy of the agro-conservation practices promoted in the demonstration plots (e.g., soil samples indicated if the soil was of higher quality; yields indicated whether crops were more bountiful as a result of interventions). Ongoing discussions with farmers, and farmer uptake of new practices, showed project team members whether the interventions were relevant and helpful to participants. Successful adoption of new practices by farm families also indicated if the proposed practices were realistic and sustainable, taking climate, economics, culture, time, effort, access to resources, and health considerations into account, within the different farming contexts. Project planning meetings, at a national and inter-national level, provided numerous opportunities for team members to reflect upon project activities. In order to understand learning outcomes from participation in the project, we conducted semi-structured interviews with participants (university collaborators, farm families, and students) to assess learning results and what had facilitated learning.

Matt, Author of Chapters 1 and 7

Assessment is the essence of teaching. The wisest person I know once said this to me and I think about it every day. As you can see from the chapters in this book and the reflections in this conclusion by some of our authors, assessment is still really all about the learner and the relationship between learner and educator. Assessment in a project-based world and a learner-centred world begins with an understanding of the experience of that learner. Who is he or she? What has brought them here? What do they value and what do they not value?

From there, assessment is the act of determining big questions, establishing learning goals, setting benchmarks, and ultimately maintaining a constant conversation between learners and educator. Yes, the final product is generally released into the ether and there is often a public exhibition, but the real determination of whether a learner has in fact learned is firmly based on the dialogue between learner and educator. As we don't often have MRI machines in our classrooms, we make these determinations of learning through conversation and observation. Was the learner able to teach new knowledge and skills to me? Have they developed mastery? Have they developed a new literacy that was not there before? Did they answer their essential question, articulating a rigorous process during which hours were spent on research and speaking with experts? Did they describe hours of revision, heartache, disequilibrium, and eventual jubilation? Did mentors in the community bear witness to their learning? And, finally, did the learner grow? Are they a different person physically, neurologically, than before?

When we consider these questions, assessment is less about marks, grades, and PISA scores. Assessment becomes a critical conversation about the development of a learner in an authentic context. In the "real world" (as if learners don't experience the real world), we don't grade our colleagues or staff. No, we coach, push, challenge, engage, and assess growth from one period of time to another based on criteria. Then we design new experiences for growth.

A myth is perpetuated out there that AP courses, exams in cold gymnasiums, and multiple-choice tests produce the conditions necessary for rigour. I get this all the time: "How does your school prepare students for the real world? For university?" Or, worse, adults – yes, adults – pass judgment on our learners and make assumptions about our school when they've never set foot in our space. But that's okay. We know, because we bear witness to it every day, that learning through projects and deep relationships with adults in the field equates to the rigour our learners yearn for. The irony of rich project-based learning, at least from the PBL perspective, is that many of our learners are already working in post-secondary institutions, working side-by-side with researchers and engaging in a mutual passion.

When I speak with learners, advisers, and mentors about their projects, and see all of them light up and become excited about their work, I see the space where learning happens. Learning – deep learning that isn't measured by cramming for an exam or by testing on information that will be lost in hours – is enshrined in relationships.

Projects are a means of allowing us the time and space to look deeply at the growth of a learner. The model for the past century has asked teachers to teach the same lesson to 120 learners without a context for creating deep relationships and for asking substantial questions. I found it difficult and often stifling to teach and learn in environments like this. In a PBL and learner-centred community, I now see learner and educator sitting side-by-side, working to create project plans, contemplating learning objectives and goals, and/or investigating the next library or expert needed for the next stage of a project. I see learners offer public exhibitions with confidence when before they were too petrified to say a word. I've witnessed learners who have fallen in love with coding, cooking, music, mathematics, art, science, and all learning as a result of being able to pursue their passion. Most of all, through projects, I have seen the greatest project of all – the flourishing of the learner. The whole learner.